MERE
FUNDAMENTALISM

MERE FUNDAMENTALISM

*The Apostles' Creed and
the Romance of Orthodoxy*

Douglas Wilson

canonpress
Moscow, Idaho

Douglas Wilson, *Mere Fundamentalism:*
The Apostles' Creed and the Romance of Orthodoxy
Copyright © 2018 by Douglas Wilson

Published by Canon Press
P. O. Box 8729, Moscow, Idaho 83843
800-488-2034 | www.canonpress.com

Cover design by James Engerbretson
Interior design by Valerie Anne Bost
Printed in the United States of America

Unless otherwise indicated, all Scripture quotations are from the King James Version. Bible quotations marked ESV are from the English Standard Version copyright ©2001 by Crossway Bibles, a division of Good News Publishers. Used by permission. Bible quotations marked NKJV are from the New King James Version®. Copyright ©1982 by Thomas Nelson, Inc. Used by permission. All rights reserved.

Library of Congress Cataloging-in-Publication Data
Wilson, Douglas, 1953- author.
Mere fundamentalism / Douglas Wilson.
Moscow, Idaho : Canon Press, [2018]
LCCN 2018024517 | ISBN 9781947644083 (pbk. : alk. paper)
LCSH: Apostles' Creed. | Catholic Church—Doctrines.
Classification: LCC BT993.3 .W55 2018 | DDC 238/.11—dc23
LC record available at https://lccn.loc.gov/2018024517

18 19 20 21 22 23 24 25   10 9 8 7 6 5 4 3 2 1

For J.I. Packer,
with thanks

CONTENTS

INTRODUCTION

THE WORD *FUNDAMENTALISM* ADMITS of many meanings, and I would like to begin by removing most of them from the table. Some of the outlying definitions would include descriptions of polygamous Mormons in the mountains of Utah, old guard members of the Politburo, radical Muslims with suicide vests in porous European cities, and very conservative Christians from the Bible belt who object to mixed-sex roller skating. What possible use is a word that puts on such an air of rigidity, but is so obviously flexible?

The word first arose in the modernist controversy in the mainline churches of North America in the first part of the twentieth century. The classical understanding of Christian theology had been eroded by the acids of higher criticism in Europe, and because conservative believers were numerically stronger in America than they were in Europe, not to mention a bit more combative, those Christians who were concerned about the rising tide of unbelief decided that a fight was in order. In response to the increase of progressive or modernist influence in the mainline churches, a set of booklets were published defending the "fundamentals" of the faith.

What these booklets were seeking to do was defend essential elements of the Christian faith, and it was an impulse that was certainly praiseworthy. When the foundations are being destroyed, what can the righteous do (Ps. 11)? The apostle Paul himself did not mind marking out certain truths as being of "first importance" (1 Cor. 15:3-4, ESV), and so there is certainly a way of emphasizing the fundamentals that is biblical and right.

But there is also a way of emphasizing these things that becomes somewhat truncated. A "lowest common denominator" mentality sets in, and pretty soon you find your list of non-negotiable fundamentals has been whittled down somewhat. The choice was presented as being between narrow and faithful or broad and faithless. Left out was the option of broad and faithful. On the practical side, in the battle between modernism and fundamentalism in the first part of the twentieth century, a battle that involved the major denominations, the big Christian publishing houses, the mission boards, and the seminaries, it has to be said that the modernists got the best of it. If we thought of it as a clash between standing armies, the armies of the fundamentalists were routed. But to simplify somewhat, after they were routed they retreated into the metaphorical hills of Kentucky and Arkansas in order to form guerrilla bands. What they retreated with—the fundamentals, a lost-cause outlook, a cultural heritage *formally* detached from Scripture, and a hardscrabble work ethic—was the raw material they used until they grew numerically strong again.

Having done so, they found themselves with a rich heritage held in a truncated way. And this is where my use of *mere* comes in. To say *mere fundamentalism* does not mean *only fundamentalism* or *just fundamentalism*. That leaves everything truncated when the need is for foundations—foundations that will eventually support a structure that is not truncated at all.

As remarked above, there are certain things in the Bible that are more important than other things. Everything in Scripture is equally *true*, but not everything is equally *important*. The fact that Jesus rose from the dead is more important than the fact that He went to Capernaum—although both are equally true.

Although it came about around 2,000 years before the phenomenon that *we* call fundamentalism, one of the best expressions of fundamentalism is found in the Apostles' Creed. There, in brief compass, we have a short statement that summarizes the glory of the

Christian gospel in a way that could be easily written on an index card, while at the same time containing vast worlds. Here it is:

> I believe in God the Father Almighty, Maker of Heaven and Earth, and in Jesus Christ, His only begotten Son, our Lord. He was conceived by the Holy Ghost, and born of the virgin, Mary. He suffered under Pontius Pilate, was crucified, died, and was buried. He descended into Hades. On the third day He rose again from the dead, ascended into Heaven, and sits at the right hand of God the Father Almighty; from thence He will come to judge the living and the dead. I believe in the Holy Ghost, the holy catholic Church, the communion of saints, the forgiveness of sins, the resurrection of the body, and the life everlasting. Amen.

Everything that matters is right here. This is because the particular truths expressed in the Creed have a universal impact and application. While this book is not, properly speaking, an exposition of the Creed, the topics addressed will have a great deal of overlap with it. And while emphasizing the importance of these crucial fundamentals, the point is not to cling to them while hiding from the forces of secularism. The Creed is not a bunker—rather it is an imposing castle on a mountain top. Every clause in it is a huge window, and so from the Creed you can see *everywhere*. The castle can be defended if attacked, but the castle is also the place from which the country is ruled. And all of it can be seen from there.

The Lordship of Jesus Christ is inclusive in one sense, but not in another. The Lordship of Christ is inclusive in the sense that nothing is excluded from its call. But in the popular senses of "inclusive religion," the Christian faith is not inclusive at all. All the nations are summoned to Christ, and all peoples stream to Him. But the invitation begins with the command to *repent*. In order to come, it is necessary to turn around and come. In order to come, it is necessary to drop what was in your hands and to come with empty hands.

Some things are shallow because they are broad, like rain water on the parking lot. Other things are deep because they are narrow, like the sliver of a crevasse that you can jump across at the top. But some things are deep because they are broad, like the roots of the Rocky Mountains.

So the title *Mere Fundamentalism* is not an attempt to whittle down the fundamentals any further. If I might speak provocatively, it is an attempt to place Christian fundamentalism in the catholic tradition. This may seem odd, but really it should be thought no more odd than placing the foundation walls under the house.

At the same time, it does requires a few words of explanation. The word *catholic* here does not refer to the Roman Catholic church, but rather to the universal Christian tradition. "Roman Catholic" is somewhat oxymoronic—catholic means universal and Rome is a city in Italy, and cities in Italy are not all that universal. At the same time, the point is not to take a jab at the communion of Rome. What we call fundamentalism has to guard against the same problem, or a very similar one. The universal truth of God cannot be held the way a sect might hold it. The truth is narrow, but the truth is never sectarian, or to be thought of as the cheat codes for a mystery religion.

Held the right way, narrow truths create the broadest of hearts. But to broaden the truth under the false guise of charity does the opposite. It is as though we could pretend that we were being ecumenical if we came to allow that 2 and 2 not only made 4, but also 3 and 5. If we were to do that, our broad truth would be in such violent revolt against the way the world actually is that we could only maintain that position by narrowing and blinding our hearts.

The way is narrow, Jesus taught, but that narrow pass opens out into a glorious mountain valley, lush and green, and teeming with game. We do not embrace that which is pinched and narrow for the sake of narrowness; narrowness is not an end in itself. Narrow is the way,

Jesus said, that leads to *life* (Matt. 7:14). He did not say that the narrow way led to being locked up in a divine broom closet. The narrow way opens out into the wide expanse of life.

When we extend the invitation to unbelievers to follow Christ, we should be doing so from that vantage of life. We are not trapped in a narrow crevasse, barely able to move ourselves, from which position we invite unbelievers to join us in our dilemma. We are not asking them to get stuck like we are. No. Humility is a low door into a high Heaven. Narrow is the pass, broad is the mountain meadow.

But we live in a generation that does not want to be precise about *anything*, and it seems that to offer them the "fundamentals," mere or not, is like offering bacon to a hungry horse. Or at least it seems that way to our inner market analyst. People just aren't interested in precise theological statements on God's triune glory, mankind's sin and rebellion, death and resurrection, and the absolute and objective truth of Scripture. But this is not exactly right—they *never* have been interested in that. In order for such things to appear to men as captivating as they actually are, the Spirit of God has to work in a way that reveals them for what they are.

Part of what we need to learn how to do is to benefit from the criticisms of our adversaries. In order to be both broad and deep, we have to be willing to see things about ourselves that perhaps only our foes can see. When evangelicals said that fundamentalists were hostile and ingrown, well, maybe there was truth in that. And when the fundamentalists said that evangelicals were just liberals in slow motion, what exactly about the last forty years would refute this? And when we appeal to the general catholic tradition, and someone says that smells and bells are next—has this never actually happened?

This book has a structure, but it is also an eclectic mix of many observations that swirl around the central themes I have chosen. If those observations help to put anything in perspective for any of my readers, then I will be most grateful.

So the thrust of this book is that just as there is a broad way that seems right to a man but which leads to death and destruction, so also there is a narrow way that opens up into unbelievable glories. This is the romance of orthodoxy. But in order to be ushered into that romance, you will have to bear with me for a little.

BEFORE THE BEGINNING: THE TRIUNE GOD

IN ORDER TO TALK INTELLIGENTLY about the Christian faith, we must always begin with God. But this does not mean beginning with God as we imagine Him to be. If we were to do *that*, we would be simply beginning with our own imaginations, and that is just another way of saying that we are beginning with ourselves. That way has always been fruitless, as many of us have already discovered. If we begin with the authority of our own imaginations, we have simply deified ourselves, which is just another way of saying that we are all still lost in a world of hurt. Our untethered imaginations have never been friends to us.

But neither may we begin with God as He is in Himself. God dwells in unapproachable light, and

whatever else this means, it means we cannot approach it. We do not and cannot know God as He is in
Himself—we cannot know God as He knows Himself. If
we knew God as He knows Himself, then we would actually be God. And if anything is true, we should know
that we are not God. If we knew God as He knows
Himself, we wouldn't be as lost as we are. If you knew
God as He knows Himself, you certainly wouldn't have
picked up this book.

Only one option remains if we are to make any
true progress at all. We must know God as He *reveals*
Himself to us. If there is an infinite chasm between us
and God, and if the chasm is to be crossed, it will have
to be crossed from His side to ours. On this side of the
chasm, as already noted, we have nothing but our own
imaginations. On the other side of the chasm . . . well,
we can't talk about that intelligently because we are all
on this side of it. If the chasm is to be crossed, then God
must cross it. He must reveal Himself.

But the word *reveal* is important. When God reveals
Himself, He is not casting shadows on the wall, or dis-
playing Himself to us in a series of intricate and compli-
cated disguises. The God who is fully known only to the
Spirit of God is *the same God* as the one who is revealed
to us. In the revelation of Himself, God is revealing, not
hiding. He is revealing, not lying. He reveals Himself; He
does not pretend to reveal Himself. A manifestation of

God that is not God Himself would be simply one more phenomenon on this side of the chasm.

And this is why we must start our discussion with Jesus Christ. The starting point must be Immanuel, which means "God with us." God is not here with us, which is why God must come here to us.

The principal way that God reveals Himself is through Jesus of Nazareth. If we come to the Father, we must come through the Son. If we have the Son, then we have the Father also. But there is some trouble in that verb *have*—how can we "have" the Son? Jesus lived a long time ago. We don't know what He looked like, despite valiant efforts by the makers of icons and Bible story books. None of us ever had a conversation with Jesus. How can the Son, someone we never met, bring us to the Father, also someone we never met?

In order to answer this question, we need to spend a few moments thinking about the *nature* of the chasm that separates us from God. There are two ways to understand this, and many people misunderstand the nature of our dilemma at just this point.

Some might want to say that this chasm exists between God and man simply because God is infinite and man is finite. In other words, some think we are necessarily separated from God simply because we are *created*. But when the Lord walked with Adam in the cool of the day, there was perfect fellowship between them even though Adam was

finite and God was infinite. There was no chasm. Adam
did not yet have union with God, but he did have complete
fellowship with God. That union will be something we discuss a bit later, but Adam's lack of it was not a problem. It
was only missing because it was not time yet. In the mean-
time, finite Adam lived in unbroken fellowship with God.

Many do not realize that part of what it means when
we are told that mankind, male and female both, is created in the image of God is the fact that we were *created* for
fellowship with God. Union with Him was a design feature from the beginning. God intended to have perfect
fellowship with finite creatures. Every creature is finite,
by definition, and it was God's intention to be united
in fellowship with us as the finite creatures that He fashioned in His own image.

And so this leads us to face up to the true nature of
the chasm between God and man. The name of that
chasm is sin. Our problem is not that we are finite, but
rather that we are rebellious. If finitude were the problem, then clearly the problem is someone else's fault.
We clearly had nothing to do with the fact that we are a
teeny little bit of matter on the face of the cosmos. We
can't help being *small.*

But the problem is not that we are small. The problem is that such small beings have such a large view
of themselves. We think that we have the right to be
our own gods, our own law, our own standard. We are

rebels. The ocean of all that exists is immense, massive, astonishingly large, and we are small flecks of foam on one part of one wave of that great ocean, and we have had the conceit to declare our independence. It is not sinful to be small, but it is very sinful to be this small and to think you are all that big.

Because God made us, and because we have sought to deny His resultant authority over us, we have thereby created the chasm that exists between God and us. The name of the chasm is impudence and folly. Another way of saying this is that the chasm is moral and ethical, not (as the philosophers might put it) ontological. The problem is not with what we are physically, but rather with the way we act morally. The problem is in our heart, not in the limited number of our molecules.

And so we should come back to the revelation of God in Jesus Christ. We should do so with this understanding of the moral nature of our rebellion in the forefront of our minds. The first thing that confronts us in any real encounter with Jesus is that He was like no other man that ever lived. He alone is good. Not only is He good, but He is good all the way through, all the way down. We encounter in Him something we have never encountered in a pure form anywhere else in the world. What we encounter in Him is holiness.

And we are simultaneously attracted to it, and repelled by it.

We know that no man ever spoke the way this man spoke. We know that He was good. We also know that no one is good but God alone. However, God is infinite, and this man, however remarkable He was, was finite. What are we to do with this?

And this, actually, was the dilemma that the early Christians faced as they were trying to puzzle through who Jesus was. They knew that the Creator God was transcendent, not contained by the world. They knew that they were sinful, incapable of finding their way back to God. They knew that someone had appeared in the middle of our history, and that He was so good, so righteous, so holy, that He obviously had to be murdered by the authorities. Our rulers murdered Him because we didn't want to be shown the way back to God, and yet through that murder, we were shown the way back to God. We will talk about the deep ramifications of that murder later. But for now we need to confront what the presence of Jesus Christ in our midst actually meant.

I said earlier that Jesus was *Immanuel*—that is to say, God with us. But how can the infinite be *with* the finite? Think of fitting the Pacific Ocean in your coffee mug, and that will give at least *some* sense of the problem. Jesus would say things like, "he that hath seen me hath seen the Father" (John 14:9). He said, "Before Abraham was, I am" (John 8:58). I AM was the great Hebrew name for God, the name that was given to Moses at his commission when he was sent back to Egypt in order to set the people free (Ex. 3:14).

The apostle John tells us that Jesus was the light that came into the world (John 1:9). This was a light that could only shine from a man, but if it were from a man such as *we* are, there would be no way it could shine. The human race is a dark star. This was the light that brought light to every man. Something profoundly mysterious was going on here.

Jesus did not put on human nature as an external sort of thing, the way a man might put on a gorilla suit. No, Jesus shone the light of God from a true human nature, from a man. Jesus did what He did as a Spirit-anointed man. He did not do miracles because He was God "inside," in a way that enabled Him to cheat.

The Lord said that if we saw Him, we had seen the Father. At the same time, everyone who saw Him saw a man. The ancient Christians puzzled it out this way. They said that Jesus of Nazareth could only be "accounted for" as someone who was fully God and fully man. He was not partly God and the rest of Him man, or partly man with the shortfall made up by God. No, He was fully God and fully man, and He did this as a fully integrated human being. He was not divided. He was not schizophrenic. He was Jesus of Nazareth.

Fully God and fully man. God in every sense, and man in every sense, and yet just One Person.

This much they affirmed, but they were careful not to talk nonsense and then call it a "religious mystery." That which was true of His divine nature could be attributed to the person Jesus of Nazareth. That which was true of His human nature could also be attributed to the person Jesus of Nazareth. But that which was attributed to the divine nature could not be attributed to the human nature, not unless you wanted to start drawing round squares.

Now I said earlier that one kind of chasm between God and man did not need to be crossed. The metaphysical distance between the Creator and a creature is necessarily infinite, and it is quite possible for the Creator to *fellowship* with any of His creatures. Whenever He creates a sentient creature, the distance is one that can be spoken across, and can be spoken across in love. The hymn writer referred to this kind of thing when he referred to a newly created member of the heavenly host. "In vain the first-born seraph tries to sound the depths of love divine." The Creator God can create a finite being and love that creature, and the finite being can love Him in return.

But more was involved in the creation of man than God creating us to fellowship with Him. The point of our creation was our eventual *union* with Him. This is part of what it means to be created in His image. So when Jesus took on human nature, and united that nature to the divine nature in One Person, He was accomplishing this ultimate purpose. The first thing Jesus did was overcome the barrier established by sin, and the second thing He did was make it possible for finite (and forgiven) beings to be united with God through Christ.

Because God has revealed Himself to us in Christ, this means that when Christ revealed the Father, Christ was here and the Father was in Heaven. As the revelation of the Father, Christ presented Himself to us as the way to the Father. And as He said, if we saw Him then we had seen the Father.

If a homely illustration may be permitted, the Father is where we need to go, the Son is the way we take to get there, and the Holy Spirit is what enables us to travel. The Father is the city we are driving to, the Son is the road, and the Spirit is the car. But we are not to think of them as three gods, or as though we were traveling from one god to another. No, the Christian faith is monotheistic. We live and move and have our being in Him, which means that we approach God by means of God in the power of God—and there is only one God. We come *to* God *from* God *in* God.

Our basic separation from Him, the separation that Christ principally overcame, was a condition of moral estrangement. Having accomplished a reconciliation there, He also ushered us into a true union with God through His incarnation, and the resurrection of that incarnate body. Jesus was raised to life for our justification. In the resurrection, we see that the incarnation was not a temporary excursion. It was not as though God decided to spend 33 years as a man, and then back to the way it was before. The life of Jesus on earth was not an instance of God temporarily slumming on earth. No, when Christ took on human nature, He did so *permanently*. And the resurrection was the seal on that permanence.

The moral separation between us and God had been a true separation, one that would end for us at the only logical conclusion, which would be the damnation of the outer darkness. The separation of spiritual death would lead finally to the second death of the final separation. This threatening gulf was crossed by the death of Jesus on the cross, when He died under the wrath of God that was due to us on account of our sins.

But the separation that existed prior to the Fall, the creational separation prior to us being invited into the life of God, was a probationary separation only. In other words, Adam was created in fellowship with God, and had he not sinned, he would eventually have been invited further up and further in. That invitation would have included true union with God. Because our race fell into sin first, before God could proceed with that plan (which had been His plan all along) He had to deal with the sin first. Then having done so, He then invited us once again to come further up and further in.

Even though we have now been granted union with God through Christ, we still remain finite. God is still the Creator and we are still creatures. Through union with Christ we have been brought near to God. So finitude is not our problem and never was.

So God the Father is the source of all. He is the everlasting and eternal Father, and He has always begotten the Son. The Son once begotten is the express image of His Father. The Father loves the Son and the Son loves the Father, and as we are talking about the love between two infinite Persons, that love is Himself a Person. This Holy Spirit is called, in various places, the Spirit of God and also called the Spirit of Christ.

Another way of thinking of this, a way suggested to us in the Scriptures, though not as common, is to think of God the Speaker, God the Spoken, and God the Interpretation. God the Speaker is the source of all. God the Spoken is the all that comes from that speaking Father. And just as no one knows the heart of a man but the spirit of the man, so also no one knows the depths of the Godhead but the Spirit of God, which means that He is the Interpreting One.

This is the God we have come to, and the point of union we have been given in Him is found at the junction of God and man—the man Christ Jesus. This is emphasized in Scripture. According to His human nature, Jesus was a Davidson. He would have been found in the phone book under the D's. According to His divine nature, He was declared to be the Son of God by His resurrection from the dead. These two natures were conjoined in the greatest miracle ever accomplished, and the result of that conjoining was Jesus of Nazareth. God did this stupendous miracle, but He did it hidden in the depths of Mary's womb. No one saw what theologians call the hypostatic union take place. It was the miracle of miracles, and it was also done completely out of sight. And so God used another great miracle to testify to the reality of this first one. God brought Jesus out of the womb of death in order to demonstrate who it was that had been conceived in the womb thirty-three years before.

THE BEGINNING:
CREATION

SOMETHING IS ETERNAL. SOMETHING
has always been and always will be. Nothing comes from
nothing, and since we are looking around at a great deal
of something, all around us, in every direction, then
something must have always been.

The question before us therefore concerns whether
that everlasting something is personal or impersonal.
Another way of putting this is that either *something* or
someone is eternal. There are really only two fundamental
alternatives before us. Either time and chance acting on
matter is the ultimate reality, or the cosmos is contingent and created, and it is here because God put it here.

Another way of thinking about this is to say that whenever we are looking around ourselves, we are looking at

that which is eternal, *or* we are looking at something that is present with us because it was created and placed here by the One who actually is eternal. However, as stated above, something is eternal.

So while we are discussing this, it makes no sense for the one who disbelieves in God to object on the basis of His self-existence because *that* particular attribute must be located *somewhere*. Ultimate reality is self-existent; the question concerns *where* this ultimate reality of self-existence should be located, not *whether* it should be located somewhere.

The position of believing Christians is that the first words of the Bible provide an admirable answer to this question. *In the beginning God created* . . . What this means is that there is an infinite divide between that which is the Creator and that which is created. In this view, God is self-existent; the heavens and earth are contingent. It is conceivable that the cosmos might not be here. God might have decided not to make it, and us. It is *not* conceivable that God might not exist—one of His names, among many others, is that of the self-identifying *I AM*.

We should not be misled by careless use of the word *God*. There are conceptions of godness that don't really take into consideration the importance of this Creator/ creature divide. For example, if someone assumes that the natural order is the body and that this body has a soul—which he would like to call god—his is a conception that doesn't take this division into account. There is only one thing, and god is part of that one thing. There is no divide, but if we imagined a divide for a moment, this god would be here in our side of it.

One writer has helpfully noted that there are two basic alternatives. Either everything is fundamentally *one*, or everything is fundamentally *two*. If everything is one, then either there is no god (naturalism) or the god of the whole show is *inside* the whole show, contained within it. If everything is fundamentally two, this means that the created order is one of those two things and the other is the eternal and everlasting God. If all is one, then that means that if there is a god, he is simply the apex predator at the top of the food chain, something like Zeus, or it is an emergent spiritual force or soul to the whole thing. But however it is configured, this god, this spiritual force, is somehow down here with us.

In this scheme, there is one great ocean of being, and that is all there is. In an ocean of being, we will not be surprised to find one of the entities within it as necessarily the biggest one within it. The ocean of being has a whale in it, swimming around near the top. We would be something like the krill. Or in another scenario, the whale might be friendlier than that. But in any case, it is possible for every entity to say to any other entity that "we are all in this together."

This is part of what modern people mean when they say that they are spiritual, but not religious. They mean that they believe there are some funny things going on in the world—maybe forces in crystals, maybe fairies in the garden, maybe a life energy in their chakras—but at the end of the day they are talking about this world containing more oddities than perhaps some scientists have recognized. But all said and done, these oddities are part of this world.

The Christian conception is quite different. The God of the Bible is fundamentally other, profoundly distinct. He has the same kind of relation to the cosmos that a painter does to his painting, a novelist to his story, an inventor to his machine. In fact, to have recourse to the biblical image, He is the potter and we are the clay.

God is the absolute fact. We are taught in Scripture that God is a Spirit, but this should not be taken—as many in fact do take it—that He is somehow a nebulous generalization. If this universe is a created thing, as it is, it *dimly* reflects the nature of the One who made it. This means that all the things within it do the same. But when we look at crab nebulae, or periwinkles, or waves on the beach, or antelopes, or lumps of coal, we are looking at concrete and very particular things. This particularity, the facticity of such things, is a dim reflection of God as the most real entity that ever was or ever could be. God is the absolute fact.

All the things we see and deal with daily are real things that aspire someday to reflect more of the absolute reality than they are currently able to do.

Some of the classical definitions of God—which when rightly understood make up the romance of orthodoxy—have been grievously misrepresented by some of their ostensible friends and dishonest foes, with the end result that we find ourselves thinking about a God who is omni-bound. This is the same thing as muscle bound, only way bigger. But God's omniscience is no frozen stare. His omnipotence is not off to the side trying to create a rock that He can't lift. And His omnipresence is not like pie dough, where the farther you spread it the thinner it gets.

When we come to grips with the fact that God created the cosmos, a corollary of this is that the cosmos is *itself* a fact. It is kind of just sitting there. As a fact, it needs to be accounted for. As one philosopher put it, "Why is there something, rather than nothing at all?" That is an excellent question, Tommy.

This is why the Christian answer seems so odd. Do you mean to say that God just *put* it here? Six thousand years ago? This raises our discomfort levels considerably. If we could just get that raw act of creation into the *ancient* past, maybe it wouldn't creep us out so much. A recent creation is almost *yesterday*, and since Adam was apparently writing things down shortly after they happened, this means there really is no such thing as *prehistoric*. A prehistoric past would be a vast unknown in which we could postulate all kinds of marvels happening all by themselves, and in addition such a vague past serves as a buffer between us and the effrontery of raw creation. But it is He that has made us and not we ourselves. We did not, and could not have, fetched ourselves out of the primordial slime by lifting ourselves by our own bootstraps. Amoebae don't have boots, for starters. Moreover, they never did.

So the doctrine of creation is a raw fact. The God who created all things as recorded in the book of Genesis is right *there*, and we struggle to accept it. If He did something back in the mists of time immemorial, then we can relegate the whole thing to the philosophers and metaphysicians. We can stuff it, in other words. But if He—approximately six thousand years ago, give or take a couple of weeks—made the aardvarks and anteaters, and little yellow canaries, and giraffes, and koala bears, pretty much as we see them today, then we have to come to grips that we are living in a place *designed* for us, and that we are responsible to the One who put us in this place that was designed for us.

The fact that we are living in a designed environment is obvious to anyone who gives it a moment's serious reflection. The only problem with the phrase *intelligent design* is that it is one of history's most grotesque understatements. The design is so apparent that *evolutionary* nature documentaries cannot go for more than ten minutes without telling us how nature designed *this*, or orchestrated *that*. In order to do his work, the evolutionary biologist has to assume the presence of intelligent design (so that he can look for it) much like a theater-goer has to engage in the willing suspension of disbelief in order to enjoy the show. If the patron of the theater were consistent with what he believes, he wouldn't pretend for a moment that the painted backdrop was a castle. In the same way, an evolutionary scientist wouldn't pretend for a moment that all these parts go together in one functioning and irreducible complexity, for there is no *a priori* reason to believe that it should.

The reason why thinking men and women deny the creation is because that is the only way to deny the Creator. If they could have design without a designer, they would take that because it would make many of their scientific problems so much simpler. But this they cannot do. There is no way to have law without a lawgiver, design without a designer, engineering without an engineer, creation without a Creator. And so they opt for the incredible hypothesis that the immense complexity that we call organic life managed to fall *up* the stairs, assembling itself as it went. The whole thing is beyond ridonkulous.

You cannot have words without a speaker, and you cannot have knowledge without someone who *knows*. The apostle John tells us that in the beginning was the

Word, but our studies in genetics have also shown us that at the *bottom* is the Word. We descend to study our strands of DNA, those random loopings of happenstance down in our genetic basement, and we have discovered vast libraries down there. Not only do we have words, we have puns and palindromes. The genetic code does one thing when you read it this way, and it is just as full of authoritative information if you read it backwards the other way.

The facade of "chance" is maintained through a severe policing of the academic community, fiercely guarding the institutions and journals that dispense scientific respectability. This is not because of a shared commitment to a search for the truth, whatever it may be, but rather to maintain their form of what one writer has called "plausibility structures." These are the unquestionable axioms that are presupposed by every secularist member in good standing. Evolution is simply *true*, and only a gibbering fundamentalist would think to deny it. Every community has these plausibility structures, but communities that are founded on dogmas that are demonstrably false, operating right alongside their formal commitment to demonstration as the ground of all truth, are necessarily brittle. Their security guards can get downright testy.

It has been quite a shock for them, understandably. If you believed that you lived in a cosmos made up of time and chance blindly acting on matter, and this has to include all organic matter, then what sensations might you have experienced if you descended down to the *tiniest* particles of this organic matter and discovered . . . *libraries*? And how are these libraries structured? Well, dear reader, if we were to take one strand of your DNA all coiled up like it usually is, you wouldn't be able to see it. It could fix comfortably under any one of the periods on this page. If you uncoiled it, it would be just over a yard long. How does it not get tangled? We have enough problems keeping one orange extension cord untangled in the garage over the winter. And this microscopically slender strand has the equivalent of the Library of Congress coded on it. Things would be bad enough for the secular evolutionist if he had gone down to the cellular basement level and just found a simple *No Smoking* sign. But no, God put *libraries* down there, and every cell in your body has one. And you have about 100 trillion cells in your body. Trillions of duplicate libraries, and that's just one person. And then we have billions of people, all with different libraries. Trillions of them.

This rapidly gets us to the point where it seems that God is just taunting us, the same way He treated Job at the end of that book. *Tell* me since you know so much. Suppose we hadn't found a whole library. Suppose we just found a short lyric poem. But *this* poem is a palindrome—if you read it backwards, it is *another* poem. And then somebody discovers that if you read every third letter, it is yet a third poem. This is the kind of genetic complexity and design that is on display every direction you look in that microscopic world. And the secular evolutionist, a self-avowed *rationalist*, continues to maintain that this palindromic poem was carved on the head of a pin by random material forces jostling around down there.

Many of us are not careful enough on the subject of information. The secularists know the universe is a big place, and that—provided there is someone available to think it—the amount of information that could be generated about the cosmos is equally vast. There is an enormous amount of information *about* the universe. And because organic life is in that cosmos, right alongside the inorganic matter, this is equally true of life. A lot can be said about it. But when we get to organic life, there is more going on. When we are talking about DNA, we don't just have information about matter that an outsider might discuss—we have matter that *has* information. Matter possesses, contains, and displays this information. We are not just talking about what we can say about what the matter just did—the way trigonometry could help us describe a rock bouncing down a hillside. Rather, we can look at a strand of DNA and, having broken the code, we can now read what that little pin prick of matter declares that *it* intends to do. And what it is going to do is build a linebacker for the Seattle Seahawks.

Creation shouts. Creation cannot really be muffled. Creation does not whisper. Day after day pours forth speech. And this is why, if we are to be creationists at all, we have to be prepared to speak into the microphone. There is really no other way to be a creationist.

This is why, once you have acknowledged the bare fact of absolute creation, the problems of a young earth fade to almost nothing. The only problem with a literal six-day creation is how it possibly could have taken so long. One of the reasons we want millions of years to process everything is that we don't want to deal with the raw sovereignty on display when God simply *creates* a male peacock—in a display not only of divine sovereignty but also of dubious taste. Completely overdone. We will not even consider the hinder parts of the baboon.

We are busy trying to hide from the gaudiness and grandeur, and this is very difficult to do. If these things eked themselves into existence over millions of years, that means we can make the mental tricks and adjustments to just take it all in stride. Millions of years is the solvent we use to try to assimilate the starkness of everything. In this attempted adjustment, everything is all arising from within "what already is," or what seems to be. Extended periods of time do not really solve the actual problem, but they do solve the apparent problem. The apparent problem is that we cannot account for all the staggering impossibilities assembling themselves into intricate organisms of exquisite design, and so we sweep our helplessness under the carpet of aeons. The actual problem remains exactly what it was before, only compounded by time. If it is impossible for me to walk across a backyard swimming pool, I cannot solve this problem by inching out onto the surface of the pool very, very slowly.

But if God just does it—*blammo*, so to speak—we have to deal with the brute facticity of what He has done. He just made up the beluga whale, and also the palm tree with the funny leaves and coconuts up on top, and the monarch butterfly which spends multiple generations flying away from Mexico in order that the descendants might all fly back to Mexico, and we must not forget the humble armadillo and the haughty camel. We cannot hide from the grandeur—grandeur radiates from the created world like heat from a wood stove. God is constantly shouting at us, but we would prefer to be deaf.

Creatio ex nihilo is a fancy way of saying creation from zip, zilch, nada, nuffin, and is therefore a foundational doctrine. On top of that it is an in-your-face doctrine. If we cannot deny it outright like some militant atheist, we would still like to background it somehow. The mists of antiquity are most convenient to us for this reason. If we cannot have the moment of creation be non-existent, we would very much like for it to be prehistoric.

This is why *young* earth creation is actually something of a misnomer. Suppose another ten thousand years go by—will it still be a young earth creation *then?* At some point it will cease to be that, but it can never cease being an historic creation, creation with a date. Whether Archbishop Ussher was correct in arguing that creation occurred in the fall of 4004 B.C., *whenever* it happened (around that time), it was a particular season in the northern hemisphere. The earth was at a particular place in its circuit around the sun, and the earth was tilting toward the sun or away from it. We don't know what day it was, but it *was* a particular day, counting back from yesterday. God knows what day of the week it was. We don't know what season it was in the northern hemisphere, but it was one of them. Creation is a fact of history.

Creation is the first *historical* moment.

THE TRUE IMAGE: MANKIND

MAN WAS CREATED IN ORDER TO FUNC-
tion as God's steward on earth. In the previous chapter we were considering the raw fact of creation. Now
we may turn to the *way* in which the heavens and earth
were called into existence, and how they were set in order once they had their being.

In the beginning, famously, God created the heavens
and earth. He spoke and the world *became*. He said the
word, and the world took shape. In the first moments after
matter and energy were created, the world was shapeless,
and needed to be molded, carved, and then sandpapered.

God shaped by dividing. He divided the heavens
and earth. He divided the evening and morning. He divided the sun and moon. He divided the land and sea.
He divided man and woman. Underneath it all, like

a rhythmic bass line, the evenings and mornings kept recurring, marking each day. His image was fully manifested to us in this final division: "So God created man in his own image, in the image of God created he him; male and female created he them" (Gen. 1:27). So we begin with the fact that He is the one who made us, and we did not make ourselves. We did not fashion ourselves. We did not invent ourselves. We also begin with the recognition that He created us *ex nihilo*, from nothing, which means that creation, by its very nature, must be *sudden*. It means that God created from scratch—more than from scratch. From nothing. This means that creation is utterly contingent. It means that the world is God's "spoken world," resting for its continued existence entirely on the sustaining word of the one who brought it into existence in the first place.

The pattern that God followed was creation, division, then reunion in a higher form, followed by yet another division. When He brought our race into being, God created Adam—which is the Hebrew word for *mankind*. When God was looking at the man He had just created, He was looking at a solitary bachelor, and alone among all the things He had fashioned, He said that this masterpiece was "not good" (Gen. 2:18). It was *not good* . . . that man should be alone. The *not good* here in this place doesn't mean defective, but rather lacking. The *not good* here means *not quite done*.

And so Adam was put into a deep sleep, into a death-like coma, and God operated on him. One was broken into two, and the bloody rib was transformed into a woman. One was made into two in order that those two could, in a different manner, become one again. And after they became one flesh, one of them, the woman, would conceive and *she* was the one who would become two. For this cause, it says, a man will leave his father and mother, cleave to his wife, and the two will become one flesh. Two become one, and then one of them becomes two. And then the cycle repeats, as it has down to the present.

As God placed the man and woman alongside one another, He was showing us an icon, or an image, of Himself. When Jesus taught on divorce, He argued from the realities displayed by the first couple, and set them forth as a paradigmatic example for all human couples to follow. This is the template that must be followed until the end of the world. With regard to divorce, the Lord said from the beginning it was not so. There was no divorce in the Garden, He taught, and so we should fight against divorce among His followers—those who are engaged in the task of re-cultivating the Garden.

God did not create two men, and so homosexuality is excluded. He did not create Adam and three women, and so polygamy is excluded. A helper suitable to Adam was not found among the beasts, and so bestiality is excluded. He did not create two women, which rules out lesbianism. All such images would be caricatures of God, and not, as He intended, the image of God Himself. In the image of God He created them, male and female created He them.

As mentioned earlier, the notion has gotten around that the image of God in man consists simply of man's reason—as though it were a simple matter of smarts. But there are many creatures that are reasonable, intelligent, smart, and not created in the image of God. There is no reason to believe that the celestial beings that inhabit the heavenly places have a low IQ. But they were not created in the image of God. God is fully capable of creating sentient beings who are a thousand times smarter than we are, and who yet do not bear the image of God. Reason is *part* of the image of God in us, but that is not what the image consists of.

We are given an indication of what is meant by the image of God in Ephesians, where the apostle Paul talks about the restoration of the image of God that is being accomplished in Christ. If the fall of man into sin had accomplished the wreckage of that image, then the restoration project that God undertook in and through Christ had to be a restoration. And that meant—if the restoration was to be conformity to Christ—that the original fall had been away from the pattern that was Christ.

We know that man and woman together constituted the image of God. When they fell, that image was damaged and vandalized, but not annihilated. After the Flood, when God required capital punishment for murder, He did so because man was created in the image of God. This meant that the image was still there to be respected, however damaged it had been by the fall into sin. So when God undertook the restoration of that image, He was not doing so from scratch. This was a remodel project, not a complete do-over.

So then we can tell something of what the original design was from the direction that the remodeling project took. One of the questions that theologians like to ask is whether the Incarnation of the Son of God would have taken place if Adam and Eve had not fallen into sin. This is not the trifling question that it might appear to be at first glance. It has to do with the definition of true mankind. We know, since the momentous events of what happened at Bethlehem, that the true definition of mankind is found in Jesus Christ. He is the ultimate and final man. The difficulty is found in supposing that another definition, a definition other than Christ, would have been ultimately possible had Adam not sinned.

Now of course, an Incarnation in a sinless world would be hard to envisage. There would have been no cross, no burial, no resurrection. Death for *sin* would have been entirely unnecessary. There would be no need for forgiveness and consequently there would be no need for the excruciating death that was the atoning basis for all forgiveness. So the Incarnation is the basis for our understanding of gospel, and gospel presupposes a fallen race. But just because the *gospel* would be unnecessary in an unfallen world does not mean that an Incarnation would also have been unnecessary in an unfallen world. Christ is the end of the law for all who believe. He is the end of the gospel as well. Why wouldn't He be the end of all *life*, regardless of what happened at the tree of the knowledge of good and evil?

I mentioned a moment ago that this work of salvation was a remodel project, and not a new project starting from scratch. And this means that the original blueprints were never scrapped. The point was to reverse the damage that had been caused by sin, the effects of the vandalism, and then to resume the project. We have some indication of some of the elements of the original when we look at what God is after in the restoration. In Ephesians, Paul says this: "And that ye put on the new man, which after God is created in righteousness and true holiness" (Eph. 4:24). The process of sanctification is the process of putting on the new man, who is Christ, thus abandoning the ruin created by the old man, who is Adam. When Paul notes the template being used here, he mentions two words—righteousness and holiness.

The meaning of history can be summed up with this one question—"What shall man be like?" The Fall was a rejection of the original plan, an attempt on our part to strike out on our own. The attempts to create a superman have not been few. We see it in the attempt by the antediluvians to breed immortals (Gen. 6), we see it in the ravings of Nietzsche, and we see it with modern unbelievers tinkering around with the human genome. In reply, God says—God has always said—that mankind shall be like Christ.

The creation of man was the creation of mankind in embryo. It did not yet appear what we would be like. The Fall into sin was an alternative proposal—as though a human child in the womb had the suggestion made to it that he try to grow into a penguin instead. The results were appalling, neither one nor the other. The results were a wreckage. God promised very early on that He would intervene at some point in the future, and that He would intervene in such a way as to put us back on the original plan. The coming of Christ accomplished two things therefore—it dealt with the rubble of the ruined first cathedral that was lying all around, cleaning up the mess, and it got the construction of the cathedral back on track. This was to be the same cathedral in the foundational ways, but it was also to be a far more glorious cathedral.

Why this talk of a cathedral? Another word used in close association with this theme is the word *glory*. Just as woman is the glory of man, so also man is the image *and glory* of God. The destructive effects of sin are seen in how it causes us to fall short of the *glory* of God. Sin is a glory failure. Those who are to inherit eternal life are those who seek for *glory*, honor, and immortality, as Paul notes in Romans 2:7.

The great sin of man is not ambition, but rather a wrong-footed ambition. We were seduced by an ambition that wanted to "be as God," (ASV) but which wanted to do it on our own terms. We would rather fail autonomously than succeed by grace. We would rather crow from the top of our dunghill than be lifted up to the sides of the North by the hand of a gracious, giving Father.

Mankind in the Garden was an ambitious project. It was not a perfect world, but more like a perfect staging area. The materials were being assembled. The project was interrupted right at the start, but it was not by someone or something that was simply being destructive. From the very beginning, the question was whether the world should be populated with billions of sons and daughters of God, reflecting His image more glorious with each succeeding century, or whether it should be populated by a race who owed their obedience to their father the devil.

So there were two ambitious projects—one the City of God and the other the city of man. The striking thing is that the initial twisting of God's design did not make Him give up on His project in the slightest. He was still going to do what He had always intended to do, but He was going to do it over the shattered rubble of the devil's kingdom, and He was going to raise up His final race of sons and daughters regardless. In other words, the initial twisting of God's purposes was not followed by any surrender on God's part at all. Right after the Fall, our race was promised someone, descended from the woman, who would crush the seed of the serpent. That promise is given in the third chapter of the Bible (Gen. 3:15), in the same chapter that includes the Fall, and the curses for the Fall. God had cosmic redemption on His mind from the first pages of the Bible.

The history of the world since that time has been a struggle between the seed of the serpent and the seed of the woman. The antipathy between them is settled and nothing can be done about it. People can switch sides, but they cannot make the two sides one. There is final and complete enmity between the seed of the woman and the seed of the serpent. The nature of this ongoing struggle is two-fold. One is the active struggle itself, and the other is the battle over the narrative. The first concerns the armies in the field, and the second concerns what we might call "the media." There is the fighting, and then there is the narrative about the fighting. Who wins the battle, and who controls the narrative? The answers to these questions are not always the same.

Two rival ambitions. Two competing ideals for humanity. One begins with the image of God and grows up into the image of God, fuller, more complete, glorious beyond all mortal reckoning. But underneath the whole process, behind it encouraging it on, in front of it beckoning, over it soaring, is the spirit of gratitude that is owed to God for His indescribable gift. God is incomparably sovereign, in complete control of all this, and He gives us all things to enjoy, which is why we are to live and move and have our being in a spirit of thanksgiving.

The other ambition promises a great deal, and has done so from the beginning. You shall be as God. Not only that, but you will be as God without any responsibility to give thanks to anyone. You will have done it yourself. In one way or another, the striving is always in the direction of Nietzsche's Übermensch, and it always seems to wind up as Nietzsche himself did—broken, mad, pathetic. The Ring promises us a king or emperor with godlike powers, but delivers us Gollum. The seductive autonomy, the inviting mastery, calls us to ascend the sides of the North, and there to discover fullness. But when we accept that invitation we find that we are not full at all, but have rather been stretched thin, almost transparent. Instead of the weight of glory, we find ourselves the possessors of a thin and very brittle vainglory. This happens because one ambitious vision speaks the truth, and the other one is lying to us. The true voice says that our ambition can only be realized on the other side of the grave, that death is followed by resurrection. We know that this is true because Jesus showed us the way. The other vision says that the way to eternal life is by never dying, and this is a cheat, a lie, a snare. Life that follows after resurrection is the kind of life that multiplies, thirty, sixty, and a hundred fold. Life that tries to live by stretching out the only kind of life it has ever known is a life that is barren. It withers. Death truly is an enemy, but it is an enemy that, when conquered, allows the victor to rejoice in the spoils. But the secret to killing death is that you must go *through* it. Again, Jesus showed us the way to do this.

The mystery of regeneration is not a process by which God turns us into angelic creatures or spiritual wisps. Regeneration is the process by which human wreckage is turned into humans. We are not turned into something *else*, but rather we are turned into what we were all along intended to become in the first place. It was sin and rebellion that attempted to turn us into something else, the attempt to change fundamental direction. God as our Father was the One who created us to call Him Father, and this was a design feature. In the rebellion against Him, we became, in the words of Jesus, a brood of vipers, children of the serpent, offspring of our father the devil. But we were created to be men, not snakes.

Man was created to stand upright, as one of the Puritans once noted. All the animals look down at the ground; they are anchored to earth. It is their home, and so it is no disgrace to them. But man stands upright; he was created to be the vicegerent of this world. He stands on the ground as much as the beasts do, but his eye takes in the heavens as well. He can look at the stars in the sky as easily as he can look at the acorns on the ground. He was first given dominion in what is called the cultural mandate (Gen. 1:28). He was given that same mandate again after the Flood (Gen. 9:1), and so we know that the mandate was not revoked on account of man's sinful condition. If God repeated our marching orders twice, once before the Fall, and the other time centuries after it, then this means that while our *ability* to fulfill the task might be affected by our sin, our responsibility to fulfill the task is untouched.

And what the gospel was intended to do is restore that ability to man. Our duties were unaffected by the Fall, but our ability to fulfill those duties were radically maimed. We continued to have the responsibility to "replenish the earth," but no ability to do so. This meant, in part, that man was now a stranger in his own world—created to exercise dominion, but unable to exercise dominion. Man was created for this dominion, and cannot be himself without it. And so it is that we cannot understand the nature of man without understanding the vocation of man—that, and what interrupted that vocation. And once we understand the interruption, we will be better positioned to understand the remedy.

THE IMAGE MARRED: SIN

WE HAVE ASSUMED THE FACT OF MAN'S rebellion and sin against God in the previous chapter. This was necessary because sin is so much part of our experience that it is scarcely possible to sketch mankind in any recognizable way without describing the sin also.

But at the same time we now need to consider the nature of our sin directly. Man was created for glory, and sin was thrown into his path to interrupt his approach to that glory. All have sinned, we are told, and fallen short of the *glory* of God.

So sin is inglorious. What else is it?

If we start where we ought to start, we will recognize that sin is splendid. There is a way that seems right to a man, but the end thereof is death (Prov. 14:12). Satan's messengers do not appear at our doors in the guise of ghouls and imps, promising to lead us astray. When Satan tempted the Lord, he did so—among other things—by showing Him all the kingdoms of the world, and their *glory*.

So both sides of the antithesis promise men glory. One promises a glorious fruition that follows on after the bleeding sacrifice. The other promises splendid glory now, in the present, with easy terms to be paid off later. The second approach is the buy-it-on-time approach to glory—but you can take the glory home with you now. Walk out of the store with it. The first approach to glory is the approach that saves up for it, and when you have enough money, *then* you go to the store.

The anti-glory called sin can only succeed by presenting a false front of glory. All the glory is given away at the front end, and you are left at the end of your days—as some homeless guy on the street—lamenting how much you had hated correction as a young man. But you had hated correction because it had seemed to want to bridle your strength, which is a young man's glory. The way of life, the way of permanent glory, looks and feels inglorious at first. It looks like humility and therefore smells like death to us. The glory is found in the resurrection, and faith has learned how to see that glory manifested earlier, in the kind of sacrifice that attains to such glory. In this, it is just imitating the Lord. He was the one who said that when He was crucified then He would be glorified (John 17:1-5).

A man seeking true glory has his eye fixed on God. A man in pursuit of vainglory is given to the sidelong glance. He is looking at his neighbor, either scheming how to stay ahead of him, or lamenting the fact that he is so far behind. The former simply accepts the assessment of God, while the latter is given over entirely to comparisons. If we all fail the course as determined by the instructor, the only thing left—if we must have glory, as we must—is for us to compare our failing grades against one another. One person has a 38 and the other a 49. We grade on a curve.

So the difference between righteousness and unrighteousness is the direction we are looking. If we are looking to God and His Word, then we can see Him and our neighbor accurately. If we are looking at our neighbor, we cannot see anything. This is because envy blinds. At the same time, it can see everything except for the essential point. It is a bizarre sort of 20/20 blindness.

Just as God and the devil are not opposites, so also righteousness and sin are not opposites. God can have no opposite, and yet one of His delusional celestials conceived a different possibility and tried to attain to it. But rather than becoming God's rival opposite, the devil simply became a fallen angel, a counterpart, if to anyone, to Michael the archangel.

In a similar way, sin is necessarily parasitic. Sin is *bent* righteousness. Sin cannot exist in its own name, it cannot stand on its own feet. Goodness, being an attribute of God, simply is. Evil is a knock-off, a corruption, a twisting, and a deviation. In order to arrive at sin, there has to be a *Fall*.

All sin is *a function of relationship*. This is the way it must necessarily be in that the universe is a personal place, created and sustained by a tri-personal God. Everything is personal, and this is especially the case with sin. It is not as though we live in an impersonal cosmos, with certain places, like that mysterious x on the floor, somehow "off limits." When God prohibited the tree of the knowledge of good and evil, it was not a matter of an arbitrary restriction. There was a test, certainly, but it was a test of personal loyalty.

Sin must be against someone. It is not primarily a matter of being against a *rule*—for a rule does not exist without a rule-giver, or the specified persons that the rule concerns. The two great commandments (that sum up all the law and the prophets) are commandments *to love persons*. The first and greatest commandment is to love God with all our heart, soul, mind, and strength (Deut. 6:5). The second commandment is similar. You shall love your neighbor as you do yourself (Lev. 19:18), and Jesus made it plain that your neighbor is whoever God has placed in front of you in the current moment.

So the two all-encompassing commandments are commandments that have to do with our treatment of persons. That means that all Christian ethical reasoning must be concerned with these same persons—God and neighbor. And breaking any commandment boils down to this—a refusal to love someone that we were called to love.

There is another person involved as well—the person who is receiving the commandment. If he just considered the law as a thing in itself, not related to persons, then he is simply dealing with a commandment carved into stone. And when the commandment is stone, so is the heart that thinks the command is stone. When the heart is made alive (which only God can do), then the commandment comes to life as well.

So there is God, there is the person obeying (or not), and there is the neighbor. The law, or what we call the law, is simply a description of what love between these persons looks like when it is rightly ordered. The law is not an autonomous, stand-alone entity. I cannot break the law as an abstraction, as though that is the sum of it. No, whenever the law is broken, that means that *someone* has been wronged, grieved, or hurt. Not only so, but the person doing the wrong is affected by it—he is turning into something else.

This is why obedience and disobedience are not instances of moral bookkeeping, or any other impersonal activity. It is not as though we were given a certain number of blue counters to bet with, and if we come out of this life with some counters left, we are somehow okay. No, in all our moral choices—obedience, sinning, repenting, refusing to repent, etc. we are in the process of becoming something. Or, more accurately, all of us are becoming someone.

At the end of the process, salvation and damnation will be seen as functions of fellowship or estrangement. Salvation is being in fellowship with the God of all that is, and damnation is being estranged from everyone and everything. That is why the end result of a life of sin, the final destination of all sin, is described as the outer darkness.

One of the more pathetic attempts to misunderstand this tries to make Hell sound like a place where someone can go to be "with all his friends." Hell is supposed to be the place where a man can drink beer with his buddies, and not have to spend any time at all with the pharisaical hoity toity, who somehow pulled one over on God and managed to populate Heaven. This willful misconstruing of what is actually happening is summed up nicely by Dorothy Parker's poem *Partial Comfort*.

> Whose love is given over-well
> Shall look on Helen's face in hell,
> Whilst those whose love is thin and wise
> May view John Knox in Paradise.

The pinched and miserable fill up Heaven, and the large-hearted go to Hell. This is a phenomenon that proper theologians call "wishful thinking." There will be no companionship whatever among the lost, and there will be nothing but companionship with those who are saved.

Those who are spiraling downward in the final lost-ness are people who are in the process of losing the *capacity* for relationship. Scripture describes that kind of relationship as one which bites and devours, or which wants a relationship with others so that someone might be within striking distance. But eventually everyone moves out of range for their own sake, and is angry that others moved out of range for their sake.

So the end result of this process is an endless, ceaseless gnawing, relentlessly pursued by former human beings. This process might be called the ultimate gollumization of a once noble creature. How far away from God can an imitative and reflective creature like man get and still reflect His image? What is there in the outer darkness *to* reflect?

Sin wants a private reserve, where all thoughts, in-tentions, lusts, and hatreds can be kept hidden, known only to the custodian of that private reserve. The sinner holds, or so he thinks, the key to all the locks on all the doors in the labyrinth corridors of his heart. This is, Jesus taught, the central folly of the Pharisees—He called it the leaven of the Pharisees. The antidote to that leaven called hypocrisy was the realization that there is nothing covered that shall not be revealed, and nothing hidden that will not be made known (Luke 12:2).

There must be something more to this than the threat of crowd shaming. If we were all gathered before the throne of God on the last day, and some of us were at the back of the line, it is doubtful that any of us would be craning our necks trying to pick up some choice bits of gossip from the front of the line. All of us would be occupied with other worrisome thoughts—what were we going to say when it was our turn?

Put another way, when the heavens and earth flee away, we are not going to be worried about our reputation in the abstract. That is not really what is going to happen. That is not going to be the concern.

Yet at the same time, the text says that everything is going to be revealed and made plain. The word used for *revealed* has the meaning *unveiled*, and is a word that we get our word apocalypse from. And on a personal level, it *will* be apocalyptic. Every mouth will be stopped. No one will have anything to say in their own autonomous defense. We often talk as though Hell were nothing but a gigantic miscarriage of justice, the end result of God somehow losing all sense of proportion. We want to think of the Last Judgment as requiring an impressive explanation and defense because we think of it as that day at the end of the world when God loses His temper. And wouldn't He apologize for that at some point and let everybody into Heaven?

But actually the doctrine of Hell is the doctrine of *nothing but* justice. It is nothing *but* due proportion. That's why we really don't like it.

We would like the orthodox doctrine of judgment to say something like this: "Because you committed this particular sin at Time X, God is going to apply the everlasting flames to you for Eternity Y." This would seem to be disproportionate, and this is why we want to frame it this way. We don't want the last judgment to stop every mouth. We don't want the realities of the last judgment to stop our mouths. We are modern men and want the doctrine of the last judgment to give us an opportunity to run our mouths.

But the reason Hell is eternal is because lack of repentance is eternal. The *sinning* is eternal. In other words, it is not *God* who has no sense of proportion—it is the sinner. He is the one who sinned at Time X, and who refuses to repent in humility for Eternity Y. Think of it as the everlasting sulks.

A thought experiment might help us here, one that may help us to understand the nature of sin. Suppose that a sinner in Hell were to genuinely, sincerely, honestly, and conscientiously *repent*. We know from Scripture that this will not happen, but a thought experiment can help us anyway. If it did happen, there is no way that

Hell could contain such humility. Hell is far too low for a lowly heart.

There is a mystery in lawlessness. It has been wisely and rightly said that the essence of Heaven is where we say to God, "Thy will be done," and the essence of Hell is where God says to man, "*Thy* will be done." This is not to take away from the reality of Hell as the wrath of God, but rather is to discuss the mechanics of that wrath. It is God who says, "Depart from me," and it is God who rejects the person who will not reject his own sin.

So God does not lose all sense of proportion. He excludes from Heaven only those who refuse to let go of their own wild and disproportionate sinning. God doesn't demonstrate a lack of proportion. He banishes it from His presence. That is why there is a Hell.

In the first chapter of Romans, the apostle describes the mechanics of wrath in this way. The wrath of God is visited from Heaven on all the ungodliness of men, but he does not go on to describe lightning bolts and hail the size of cantaloupes. No, the wrath of God is described as God "giving men up." Giving them to what? Giving them up to what they desire. The fact that their desires are maddening lusts does not alter the fact that God is giving them up to what they want, and to what they demand.

So damnation is not an arbitrary penalty attached randomly to certain proscribed behaviors. Rather damnation is what happens at the culmination of insisting upon a fundamentally irrational frame of mind. So it is not as though God assigns the rack to adulterers, or the thumb-screws to the forgers. And it is not even what we see in Dante, where the penalties have some sort of poetic con-nection to the sin, some sort of poetic justice involved.

Rather, on this reckoning, damnation is the consum-mation of a process, and the process has been unfolding all along. Salvation is the interruption of that process, and the radical introduction of a new process. We arrive at the last where we arrive because we have become at the last what we have been becoming all along.

To begin to get a glimmer of this shift in thinking is to realize it is not a mere "shift." This represents, if we grasp it, a Copernican revolution in our thinking. Everything is turned around. The reality of Hell is not an indictment of the justice of God; Hell *is* the justice of God. Hell is not the reality that demonstrates how unjust God is, but rather the reality that manifests how unjust we are. But before we get to that moment of reve-lation, we want to pretend to ourselves that it is all very different. We demand to know how a loving God can send anyone to Hell, when the real problem is how a just God could send anyone anywhere else.

And so we are not just arguing that the justice of God cannot allow willful sinners into Heaven, although that is true. We are also arguing that the love of God cannot

admit them into Heaven. Heaven is the habitation of all
love, and how could a loving God allow such a place to
be wrecked by people whose sense of proportion is so to-
tally skewed that they would rather be miserable forever
than to repent of the tiniest sin?

To talk about sin and Hell is like talking about acorns
and oaks. Hell is the culmination of sin, and not just
an externally imposed consequence of it. Put another
way, Hell *is* sin, but sin matured, sin come to the final
fruition of emptiness.

Later in this book, we will talk more fully about the
last things, the Final Judgment, as considered as the
"end of the world." But here we are talking about it using a different sense of the word *end*, which we have to
do whenever we are talking about sin and the individual.
What is the final end of sin, what is the *telos* of sin, what
is the point of sin?

Because it involves a rejection of God and His holy
character, that final end has to be foundationally incoherent. But to the extent it can even be understood, the end
of sin is me, me, me . . . an endless gnawing on the bones
of what is left of "me." That word would echo endlessly,
but there are no walls close enough for anything to echo.
There is hardly anything that remains to gnaw, and hardly
anyone left to do the gnawing, and what is there is residue
of human, the detritus of the image of God.

So sin in our lives now is attempted murder—where we are trying to slay the image of God in ourselves. Hell is the result of having successfully done so.

THE IMAGE RESTORED: DEATH AND RESURRECTION

GOD USES CERTAIN THEMES OVER AND over again. He tells exile and return stories. He tells underdog stories. He tells younger son stories. He tells cliffhanger stories. And He tells death and resurrection stories. Death and resurrection stories are His favorite.

But despite telling them repeatedly, He tells them in a way that prevents them from becoming hackneyed or clichéd. Perhaps it is the fact that He is constantly verging on the melodramatic, but with just enough real danger to keep our attention focused. This is the reason death and resurrection stories are always exciting. In order to follow the story, there has to be an actual *death*, and that always grips the attention. Even if the executioner is not all that competent, he still is capable of keeping your attention.

It is very easy for moderns to assume that such a doctrine of resurrection (saying that life can come from inanimate matter) is beyond fantastical. But this demeanor is not really a characteristic of the *modern* mind; it would be better to describe it as characteristic of the *unbelieving* mind, the kind of mind that has been with us in every generation. In many ways, modernity is simply unbelief in fashionable clothing. The apostle Paul ran into unbelief in ancient Athens, there encountering men who thought that the concept of resurrection from the dead was beyond crazy. They thought he was preaching foreign gods (plural) because he kept going on about Jesus and *Anastasis* (the word for resurrection). They also thought he was a scholarly nut.

But this skeptical frame of mind leaves one significant thing out of its calculations—and that thing concerns what absolutely everyone involved in the discussion already knows has happened. *Everyone* believes that living things come from dead things.

Christians believe that God fashioned Adam from the dust of the ground. Evolutionists believe that we emerged millions of years ago from the primordial goo. So both believe that animated life came from inanimate matter. Both believe that first there was *no-life* and then there was *life*. First there was *dead matter* and then there was *not dead matter*. Everybody thinks this. Christians are the ones who think it will happen *again*.

There are other obvious distinctions. Christians believe that this feat was accomplished by an omnipotent Deity, while evolutionists believe that inanimate matter somehow assembled itself into a mechanistic approximation of the élan vital.

So this means that no one is in a position to talk about this as an impossibility. Life from the dead may be described as unlikely, but we should keep in the back of the mind the fact that the unlikelihood of it is being maintained by someone who didn't used to be alive, and who is now alive, saying compelling stuff—stuff like "*That* could never happen."

If you roll the dice and double six comes up, you can get a statistician to back you up in the claim that doing it again on the very next roll is unlikely. But you can't get him to agree that rolling double six is always impossible because the die are already there on the table, looking up at the two of you. *You have already done it once*, and so we should all grant that it is not impossible.

To use another example, suppose a group of us are standing on a desert island. We have no boats, but we can see a distant island, one we have never been to, off in the distance. Someone wonders aloud if any people live on that island. Now they may or may not live there, but what would you think of one of your companions who argued the negative because, he maintained, it is impossible for people to live on islands. But, you should reply, we are people and we are on *this* island. It is obviously done *sometimes*.

Now returning to the illustration of the dice, the *likelihood* of this is affected by whether or not you are an evolutionist because as a blind process the odds of it all happening the first time were incredibly long. Twice in a row would be astronomical odds, but then . . . we were already dealing with astronomical odds. Squaring the total again makes it less likely, sure, but blind evolution doing everything it is alleged to have done the first time was already a infinitely colossal jackpot. Why not stay in the casino since we're feeling lucky?

But if we believe in a Creator, we are not talking about odds at all, but rather just a *decision*. If God decided to create us in the first place, bringing our race out of the dust of the ground, then no more is involved in the resurrection of the dead than Him simply doing it again. This is no more problematic than a man deciding one morning to go to work by a particular route, and then the next day deciding to do the same thing again. If He has the authority and power to make the decision once, and that authority and power do not disappear, then He can simply do it again.

This is another way of saying that belief in the resurrection is only "a reach" if you deny the doctrine of creation. But if you deny the existence of a Creator, this means the odds of the necessarily evolved life-from-inanimate-matter scenario are staggeringly longer odds than the Christian idea of the creation of Adam from the dust of the ground, *and* the resurrection of the dead at the end of history.

Put another way, life from the dead *once* in an evolutionist's world is far less likely than life from the dead *twice* in the Christian world. This is because we are comparing random chance occurrences to deliberate acts performed by a person, and it is like comparing apples and glaciers. The unbeliever might want to push it back a step in order to ask what the odds are of God existing, as through that were an open question. God is a self-existent being, the one who called Himself I Am That I Am, and so consequently the chances of Him *not* existing are zero. It is a simple calculation.

But here is where the trouble lies. Creation and resurrection are not the realities that unbelievers actually find incredible. Given the reality of God, those events are by no means a difficulty. All God has to do is nod, and the cosmos is *there*. All He has to do is say "Do it again," and the sea gives up her dead. The apostle once asked Agrippa this very thing—"Why should it be thought a thing incredible with you, that God should raise the dead?" (Acts 26:8). Grant the existence of God and the most astonishing things follow.

But this cannot be an argument against Him because we are surrounded by the most astonishing things

now—lady bugs, sloths, birds of paradise acting like a
goon show, and we have not even mentioned all of the
giant squid. Not only do we have thousands more examples, but we have thousands more species of examples.
Hundreds of thousands more species of examples. We
have hundreds of thousands of species of *beetles.*
What unbelievers find incredible, therefore, is the reality of God Himself. God is Life in Himself, and if that
is what He is, then He may grant life wherever and however He pleases. Acknowledge God and you find that all
else follows easily. But that, the unbeliever might say, is
just the incredible thing. God is unbelievable. God is
only unbelievable because God is unbearable—for He is
holy and we are not.

Our ability to believe in resurrection life is therefore dependent on our ability to believe in the One
who is Life Itself. Our earthly creational life, and our
resurrection in the world to come, are both gifts from
the One who is eternal and everlasting life. Deny the
headwaters of that particular river, and you still have to
give an accounting for the fact that we are here, now,
alive. And we, living beings, arrived here inexplicably,
and we emerged into a self-consciousness of that life,
along with an awareness that such self-consciousness
had to be considered to be absolutely meaningless—
which would unfortunately render our meditations on

our meaninglessness themselves meaningless. You can run but you can't hide.

What we are trying to do is fit what we observe with our eyes into a larger story. What we *assume* about that larger story is determinative. If we assume evolution, then it doesn't make sense to postulate that our particular consciousness survives death, or could somehow circle back around again, whether in reincarnation or resurrection. It would just seem like special pleading to argue that we get a second turn on this ride. But this is only because of what is assumed about the back story.

But if God created us, it makes sense to ask what *kind* of beings we were created to be. He can make us whatever shape He likes. He can make us whatever length He wishes, as measured in terms of longevity. He can create midges that live for three days and tortoises that live for two centuries. It would make no sense to say that if God is going to create us all as creatures, then He has to give us short necks. He *might* do so, but then we see the giraffes. We don't get to set down stipulations beforehand. The act of creation is necessarily an act of complete sovereignty. God could have created us with four arms if He wanted, or with two livers.

And another possibility is that we might have been created in our first earthly life to simply be phase one, a chrysalis. That is what the doctrine of the resurrection assumes.

So put another way, what kind of creatures were we created to be? The answer is that bodies were created to be *seed*. It is the nature of seed to germinate in such a way that life proceeds from life—but with a death intervening. "Verily, verily, I say unto you, Except a corn of wheat fall into the ground and die, it abideth alone: but if it die, it bringeth forth much fruit" (John 12:24). A kernel of grain can only die if it is alive to begin with, but once it has been reduced to death, life opens up again before it. Not only so, but life that is thirty, sixty, or one hundred fold *more* life.

Grant the premise and everything follows. The apostle Paul, as mentioned earlier, addressing the sophisticated Agrippa, anticipated this argument. Note the words *a thing incredible*: "Why should it be thought a thing incredible with you, that God should raise the dead?" (Acts 26:8). In other words, we have two kinds of incredulity expressed in the same passage. One thinks it is incredible that God would raise the dead, and the other kind of incredulity is amazed at the unbelief.

The difference between the believer and unbeliever *appears* at the doctrinal point of resurrection, but the real divide is found in the reality of the living God. The difference begins far earlier. If God lives, then we shall live again. We know this because God lives, and we are alive now. We are living seed, and seed cannot exist without a crop.

Every kind of seed—animals included—will produce a crop. This unfortunately includes wicked men and women. The inexorable nature of resurrection follows its logic whether or not the seed concerned loves God. Jesus explicitly teaches us that there is a resurrection of the unjust as well as that of the just. "Marvel not at this: for the hour is coming, in the which all that are in the graves shall hear his voice, And shall come forth; they that have done good, unto the resurrection of life; *and they that have done evil, unto the resurrection of damnation*" (John 5:28-29, emphasis added).

The apostle Paul refers to the same reality.

"And have hope toward God, which they themselves also allow, that there shall be a resurrection of the dead, *both of the just and unjust*" (Acts 24:15, emphasis added).

In other words, the doctrine of resurrection is not a truth that applies to good people because they are good, or forgiven people because they are forgiven. No, it applies to all people because *people are seed*.

As was discussed earlier, all of us are in the process of becoming something. What happens to the seed in this life affects what happens to the plant that grows from it in the next. To change from an image of plants growing to animals developing, this life is a time of gestation. This is the time when the birth defects—and recall that our whole race is defective—must be addressed. If we don't want to be born "that way," the correction must take place now.

Christian conversion, being born again, is the time when God is conducting pre-natal heart surgery.

Thus the fact that we live once and then live again in a more glorified form appears to have been a design feature from the beginning. There has always been a boundary intended between the first life and the second. The name of the boundary line now is "death" because we are living in a world that has crashed due to sin. In the Scriptures, sin and the resultant death are always the enemy, never a design feature.

But death appears to be the corruption of *something*, just as everything else we see in this world is a corrupt form of something. Before there was any sin in the world, before there was any disobedience—there was a form of something, of which death as we know it is the vicious analog.

Again, Adam was put into a deep coma-like state, and that type of "death" was the condition from which the first great glorification came, the creation of the woman. This appears to have been a type. The second Adam, when He died, also had a bride taken from His side (John 19:34-35).

The first bloodshed happened when God removed the rib from Adam's side in order to fashion his bride. This was a sinless world, but still there was a bloody surgery in it.

And also before there was any sin in the world, Adam saw his wife threatened by an enemy, the serpent.

Adam's duty had been to protect the Garden, and his wife at the center of that Garden, and here was a threat to the heart of that Garden. Adam's duty was somehow to interpose himself. But that involved risk.

None of these things were banished from a perfect world. Adam had a day full of troubles before he had sinned. All of this seems to indicate that had our first parents not fallen, had they not rebelled, they still would have served as seed somehow. We have two examples of this in Scripture—Enoch being one, and Elijah being the other. They passed over the same kind of threshold that we pass over when we die, but they did it without dying. They were simply translated—but they were clearly seed. Human life at its best is clearly intended to extend beyond *once*.

A moment ago, I said that there was no sin in the world, but in one sense this was strictly speaking not true. Before this was a fallen world, there were sinful actions contained within it. Sin was certainly *present* before the Fall. The serpent was sinning when he tempted our first mother, and she was sinning when she allowed herself to be deceived. And Adam was sinning when he first reached out his hand for the fruit.

But the world did not actually *fall* until mankind fell, and that did not happen until Adam actually ate the fruit. There is a difference between sin occurring in the world, and a formal rebellion being declared and undertaken by the one who had been appointed to be the steward of the world. Adam was the Head, and when he revolted, when he declared war against God, it was at that moment that the entire created order fell.

This is why the creation is groaning as in the pangs of childbirth, longing for the redemption of the children of God. When we fell into death in the rebellion of our father Adam, the created order (for which we were responsible) fell also. As we have been laboring under a curse, the ground under our feet has experienced that same curse. When we are restored, the created order will be liberated from the cycle of death and untamed entropy at the same time.

We were created to be translated, we were created to be glorified. This was always the case—we have always been seed. But now, given the deadly realities that sin has brought into the world, we are born to die . . . but still created to rise.

The design for the complete butterfly is a design that is present from the first moment the caterpillar exists—but try explaining that to the caterpillar. We have no real reason for denying that God has a much larger purpose and intention for us than is perhaps immediately apparent to us at this moment. A child in the womb knows nothing of birth, a nursing child knows nothing of running around in the yard, a toddler knows nothing of falling in love, a man knows nothing of the resurrection

of the dead. That is, he knows nothing about it unless
he is told. But when he is told, with so many marvels
already behind him, why does he find it hard to believe?

The message of the gospel is objective; it is outside ourselves. The death, burial, and resurrection of Jesus either
happened or it didn't, and if it did happen, that occurred
before any person now alive believed or disbelieved it. It
would have been true had none of us ever been born. If
it did not happen the way the gospels describe it, it would
not have started to be true later on when people started to
believe it. The truth lies outside ourselves.

But the reason preachers go out and declare these
things as the truth of God is that we want these external
truths to become internal and experienced realities. The
goal is to have a preached Christ become an experienced
Christ, and hence a saving Christ. What is it that accom-
plishes this?

The scriptural teaching is that the just are to live *by
faith*, from first to last. We begin our Christian lives by
faith, we continue them by faith, and we conclude them
by faith. Not only so, but this kind of living faith—the
only kind of faith that God ever gives us—is a faith that is
not supplemented by any other means for appropriating
the grace of God presented in the gospel. We cannot
reinforce our faith with liturgical propriety, boyish good
looks, indignant moralism, or anything else. It is not of
him who runs, but of God who shows mercy.

This is why sound theologians speak of faith *alone*. The ground of our justification is the objective truth about Jesus. The instrument, the sole instrument of our justification is the faith that God gave to us . . . and He gave that faith to us to keep us from bragging about *anything*. The one who boasts should boast in the Lord. So God gives us salvation (the death, burial, and resurrection of Jesus) and He also gives us the hand that receives the salvation (faith).

One other thing should be mentioned about faith, and I mention it because we can get ourselves pretty tangled up in this. We are saved by Jesus through faith alone. We are not saved by believing *that* people are saved by Jesus through faith alone.

Another way of saying this is that faith is passive, faith is receptive. Faith accepts. Faith *receives* the salvation, and it does so without *contributing* to that salvation. The eye receives light: the eye does not shine on anything to make it brighter.

When a man sits down in a chair, he certainly has faith in the chair. But it is the *chair* that holds him, not his faith. The faith does not provide an iota of additional strength to the chair. But the faith still sits.

Faith is the natural response to the perceived and understood faithfulness of God. And so that is why, if we want to see great faith, we should not exhort anyone to hover over their faith, trying to get it to grow.

No, faith comes by hearing and hearing by the Word of God. This means that great faith comes from the proclamation of a great gospel, a great Savior, and a great God who sent Him.

SCRIPTURE, TRUTH, AND KNOWLEDGE

THERE WAS A TEMPTATION, OF COURSE, to have the topic of this chapter be located right at the front. But I left it back here for a reason.

Modern men like to think that epistemology, the study of how we know what we know, is a fundamental subject. It is actually a realm of fundamental confusions.

If we want to discuss ultimate issues, of the sort that I have been addressing in this book, we want to start at the very beginning, and we think that the very beginning is "How we can know anything at all?" And, once we have answered the question of how we know, we ask how we can possibly know that. And as it turns out, it really is turtles all the way down.

Epistemology is like taking your eyeballs out to look at them. If your optic nerves were elastic, and you could pull your eyeballs out and point them at each other, what exactly would you see? If we settle how we know things, we have not yet addressed the question of how we know that. We are in the fun house, and it is mirrors everywhere.

At the same time, the question has to be addressed sometime. But addressing the question means putting it in its proper perspective. It does not mean flattering the pretensions of those who think that we are capable of grounding our knowledge on an ultimate foundation. All creaturely knowledge, all knowledge of finite creatures, is finite. And because our knowledge has two characteristics—it is finite and it is true knowledge—this means that it must of necessity be axiomatic knowledge. Another way of saying this is that we must reason from first principles or abandon reason altogether. If we have nowhere to stand, we are going to have trouble lifting rocks of *any* size.

Finite creatures always have to begin from somewhere. Finite creatures have to *start*. God has created us in such a way as to be able to reason axiomatically, and for that to be the only way we could be able to reason. These axioms can be of pure reason (parallel lines don't cross each other), or practical reasons (little boys shouldn't tell lies to their mothers). *Axioms do not need to be proved.* To demand that they be proved is to demand that all our philosophy departments descend into a whirl of nihilistic madness. By demanding proof for everything, we have made it impossible to arrive at a proof for anything. When you demand a proof for everything, leaving no room for the axioms that can launch you, you are automatically exposed to the cold reality that there is no way to prove that proving things proves anything.

One of the axioms that men must have in order to be able to reason is that *God is, and that He reveals Himself.* This is not the only axiom there is, but it is the most important one. The one who comes to God must believe that He exists, and that He is the rewarder of those who seek Him (Heb. 11:6). In short, we must begin with the axiom that God exists, and that God is good.

If we back away from this truth in order to examine theological claims more "objectively," we are trying to set up our libraries in the depths of some subterranean cavern with no lights, in order to read all our books *objectively.*

The primeval sin that our parents committed was spurred on with the promise that "you shall be as God" (ASV), and this is a perennial temptation, particularly in philosophy. Everyone wants to pretend that he can postulate a magic balcony upon which a finite creature can stand, and from which vantage that finite creature can survey everything in the cosmos that has any epistemological bearing or significance at all. Part of the deal is that everyone agrees not to ask too many questions about what that balcony is bolted to and what the load restrictions are.

Autonomous and humanistic epistemology is the ultimate exercise in picking yourself up by your own coat collar, lifting yourself by your own bootstraps, or standing in a bucket in order to carry yourself upstairs. Either first principles are axiomatic and self-evident, or there are no principles at all anywhere, including the nihilistic principle that there are no principles. Either we reason as creatures created in the image of God, or we are part of an endless chemical flux—having therefore no basis for believing that chemicals even exist. If a lab assistant were to spill some chemicals on the lab table and the scientist over that lab wanted to find out what happened, he wouldn't ask the chemicals. They don't know—*they* are the accident. Chemicals don't know anything about chemicals.

If we are the end product of so many years of time acting on matter as governed by chance, then we have no reason to believe any of our thoughts to be true. Our current thoughts, whatever they are, are the simple behavior exhibited by these chemicals under these conditions and at this temperature. And hence there is no reason for believing in chemicals, conditions, or temperatures.

So we must have axioms. We are finite and must have a starting point. We must begin somewhere. But is the point where we begin an arbitrary choice? May we select any random sentiment and say that since I must have an axiom, then this shall be it? "Because yogurt has no bones and the more they climb the much!" Could something like that suffice?

Of course not. Not only must we have a starting point, but we must have a starting point that does not destroy itself. If someone starts by affirming A, but by the end of our treatment of A we discover that it logically entails "not A," we don't have a need to pursue it any further. As philosophers would put it, no true statement can entail its own falsity, and it follows from this that no primary axiom can destroy itself. If it destroys itself, it is not a primary axiom.

We have already seen this with those whose axiom is a naturalistic one. If matter is all that exists, then materialism as a philosophy cannot exist for the simple reason that philosophers don't exist. *That's* not a philosopher—that's a complex chemical reaction that doesn't know what hit it. In fact, we cannot even say that it is a complex chemical reaction. We cannot get that far—we know *nothing*.

As C.S. Lewis points out in his fine book *Miracles*, we don't need to argue with a man who says that "rice is unwholesome, but I am not saying this is true."[1] We

---

1. *Miracles* (New York: Macmillan, 1947), first edition, 23-24.

needn't argue because on his terms there is no such thing as argument.

Those who hold this position are often ready to grant the radical nature of these conclusions—for the reasoning processes of every position but their own. But alas, it does not work that way. This position is a universal corrosive. It eats through every container you might want to put it in.

So this means that we may limit our primary axioms to those which do not contradict themselves—or the cosmos. Every set of primary axioms that are put forward have to make sense of the cosmos as it actually is. Put another way, we are asking what the preconditions are that would make sense of all that we actually do know.

In other words, we know the world. But given what we assume about the world, we do not know how we could possibly know the world. We do not have the preconditions of the knowledge that we know we possess. What are those preconditions?

One of the primary axioms is the assumption of the living God. There is a God, and this God reveals Himself. If He determined to hide Himself, we would never find Him. God is, and God speaks. This is a nonsensical "for instance," as we shall see in a moment.

Not only does God speak, but the Word that He speaks is the revelation of Himself. The Word of God is the manifestation of God—Immanuel, God with us.

Sophomores with two philosophy classes behind them like to pose stumpers about rocks too heavy for God to lift, as though it were nonsensical to say that there is anything God cannot do. But there are plenty of things God cannot do—He cannot lie, for instance. God cannot do anything inconsistent with His own nature and character. As C.S. Lewis says, nonsense doesn't cease to be nonsense simply because you preface it with the words "God can."[2]

And so this is why revelation is always necessary. God could not have created any possible universe that He was not God over. I am not just saying that revelation is necessary for us to know anything, although that is quite true. I am saying that God is incapable of creating a world that does not necessarily proclaim Him as the God of it. God is in fact not silent, but this involves more than that. He *cannot* be silent. His Son is the *Word*.

In any possible world, the leaves, or the mountains, or the galaxies, or the atoms, or the buttercups, all necessarily declare that God fashioned *this*. We see it clearly in the cobra and platypus, but if God had made a world full of Dr. Seuss-like creatures, they would all have proclaimed the same thing. Every contingent thing *necessarily* says that it was created and that it is currently sustained by the great God of wonders.

---

2. *The Problem of Pain* (1940; New York: HarperCollins, 1996), 18.

Another way of saying this is that natural law, natural revelation, is a necessity *in every possible nature containing sentient beings*. It does not just happen to be true in our world. It is necessarily true, in the same kind of way that summons triangles to have three sides. It could not be otherwise.

For a finite creature to assume the possibility of knowledge, knowledge of any level, without acknowledging the supremacy of the Almighty God, is an exercise in nonsense. In short, "God does not exist" is not a false statement. It is nonsense, incoherent.

All that God does He does through His executive, who is His agent. God does what He does by speaking the Word, and the Word is with Him and the Word is God. The divine action cannot therefore be silent, cannot be wordless.

Christians are therefore, of necessity, people of the Word. They are people of the Word in the first instance because they are followers of Jesus, and Jesus is the Spoken Word. They are people of the Word in the second place because God has been pleased, in every age, to give verbal expression of His will to His prophets, with clear instructions to write it down. And in the third instance, God speaks to us daily in every blade of grass, every breeze, every driveway pebble, and every crab nebula. Day after day pours forth speech, and night after night the knowledge increases. God speaks.

The believer therefore assumes that because God is the Speaker of the resurrected Word, the author of all that is, and because He has given us written instructions concerning it all, and because He is utterly, absolutely, and finally perfect, these three Words must harmonize perfectly. He needs no editor, and no second or third drafts.

To assume that these various ways God has revealed Himself—in His Son, in the Scriptures, and in the sky— could ever be placed at odds with one another is to assume a level of divine incompetence that the facts will not bear out.

When someone claims that they *do* contradict, this is generally a preface to an attempt at poor exegesis on the form of revelation they consider supreme. If they say that Jesus Himself is to be preferred (over against Scripture and natural revelation), this is likely because Jesus is about to be appealed to as the original flower child. If natural revelation is given preeminence over Christ and the Scriptures, this will probably end by appealing to evolution, climate change, and a bunch of other things that science never said. And if Scripture is chosen (over against Jesus and the natural world), this will almost certainly be the lead-in to the defense of some sort of ultra-denominationalism. But what God says *anywhere*, God says *everywhere*.

This is another form of saying that all truth is God's truth. But this saying, self-evidently true itself, has often been employed mischievously. When we say that *all truth is God's truth*, we do not mean to say that *this truth that we just thought we discovered ten minutes ago should be used to trump what we have known to be true for centuries.* That is quite a different thing.

All truth really is God's truth. But not all pretended truth is God's truth. Not all fake wisdom is God's wisdom. Not all scams are God's truth.

For example, natural revelation does not teach us that we all evolved from the primordial slime. It does teach us that homosexual relations are unnatural. The former conflicts with Genesis, and the latter does not conflict with Leviticus.

The life of Jesus does not teach us anything whatever about leftist economics. The life of Jesus does teach us how strength is true humility.

The Scriptures alone do not teach us that Antioch Lightning Tabernacle is the only true church. They do teach us God's plan of redemption for the entire world.

If you love someone, you want to read *all* the messages they send you. Some messages can be more expansive—a hand-written letter say. Some can be more restricted—a postcard. Some might be minimal—a text. But you want to read them all, and if the one who sent them all is divinely infallible, you know that the messages sent to you will all necessarily harmonize.

But they only fail to harmonize if *we* introduce the discordant elements—which we routinely and frequently do. These discordant elements can then be used by us to buffer our consciences, as we seek to keep any clear words from God getting through.

As we consider these various forms of revelation given to us, we have to recognize that of necessity we have to give the primacy to Scripture—at least in terms of our discipleship. The incarnate Word is God in the flesh, but it is through the Scriptures that we learn about Him. The natural world is eloquent, but mute at the same time. The Scriptures teach us how to read nature.

So everything always comes back to Scripture. We know how God wants us to think about everything— about Him, about His Son, about ourselves, about our sinfulness, about the world, about the Word—because *He tells us*. If He hadn't told us, we wouldn't know.

But I am saying more than simply that without His revelation we wouldn't know the content of that revelation. That is self-evidently true; it is tautological. If God does not tell us, He didn't tell us. I am making a much greater claim. If God had not given us His revelation, we wouldn't be able to know *anything*.

The history of philosophy bears this out—one epistemological dead end after another. Some philosophers think we can't know anything—while still claiming to know that. Others think we obviously know what we do, but we cannot come up with sufficient grounds for it. But we are finite. *We have to be told.* The world wants to divide our options in epistemology between rationalism, where we come to knowledge through reason, or empiricism, where we come to knowledge through our experience. But rationalism is like taking your eyeballs out to look at them, and empiricism is like rubbing your eyeballs hard until you see a kaleidoscopic light show. We are finite. If we are to know anything, we have to be told.

This is why Scripture tells us that the fear of the Lord is the beginning of knowledge (Prov. 1:7). The fear of the Lord is not the capstone to a fine obelisk that we have finally erected ourselves. It is not the final crowning achievement to all our efforts. No, the fear of the Lord is the foundation to every form of knowing. If we have the sensation of knowing without fear of the Lord, this is merely the sensation of living in a house that is built on sand as you await the coming storms. The fear of the Lord is not the object of our pursuit of knowledge. It is what makes the knowledge of anything possible.

We are finite. We must be told. And this is why we must have an infallible and perfect Word from God. This is why we must have the Scriptures.

This world is a slippery place, and the Scriptures are a rock on which to stand. This world is a dark place, and the Scriptures are the light with which we may make our way. This world is a corrupt place, and the Scriptures outline the true way of purity for us. The world is a false place, and the Scriptures tell us the truth—about God, about man, about sin, about salvation, and about revelation. The world is a seductive place, and the Scriptures speak to us in a way that reveals the vanity of it. The world is a blurry place, and the Scriptures bring everything into singular focus. The world is a distracting place, and the Scriptures bring all the right priorities together. The world is an evil place, and the Scriptures testify to us of all that is holy, righteous, and good. The world is a lost place, and the Scriptures show us how we might be used to lead the world home.

HUMANITY REASSEMBLED: THE CHURCH

THE MODERN WORLD WANTS US TO choose between the collective and the individual. We identify, by various means, either as statists or as individualists, either as socialists or as libertarians. The difficulty is that the collectivists have no bonding agent other than coercion, meaning that they can only create bees for the hive, or slaves for the erection of these impressive pyramids. And the libertarians stand for the solitary individual, atomistic and alone, utterly meaningless—and, by the way, defenseless.

In order for the collective not to be oppressive and tyrannical, it must be an organism. It needs to be *alive*. In order for the individual to have any meaning, he needs to be oriented to something larger than he is, something outside himself. But if that thing outside him is dead, then it is necessarily oppressive and suffocating.

Now the Church is a living organism, and individual Christians are members within it. The image of a living body is one that the apostle Paul used to make clear the interdependence of the individuals involved. René Girard aptly said we are interdividuals. We are not one in the way that a slab of granite is "one." Nor are we utterly distinct and separated, the same way BBs scattered over the floor would be. The slab has unity, but it is dead unity. The BBs have distinct individuality, but they are all dead individuals.

The body is not like that. The distinctions that can be drawn between the liver and the wrist, or the pancreas and the eye, are not subtle ones. These members are wildly different. But at the same time, they still share a fundamental unity within the same body.

Some parts of the body have greater honor, and some have less, but they are all distinct and important. The body of Christ has no vestigial organs, no evolutionary leftovers. God gave us a heart so that our blood could circulate. He gave us ankles so that we could walk. He gave us fingernails so that we could pick up dimes on the first try.

We have to be careful in discussing the Church. The Church is an institution in the world, but it is not *just* an institution. It can be photographed, but the life that animates it cannot be photographed. Unconverted people can attach themselves to it and partake of its life in a very limited sense, but they have no ownership in that hidden life that makes the Church what it is.

The Church can own property and can build buildings. In fact, those buildings can become so associated with the Church in the minds of the public that they point to it and say, "That's a church there." But that is just the part of the Church that keeps the rain off the saints. The Church can be written into political constitutions, and pollsters can interview the people who go to a church.

But the true internal center of the Church is the Holy Spirit, who is the Spirit of life. In a world filled with death and corruption, the Holy Spirit hovers over the face of the sewage lagoon, brooding on the face of the waters. And there, in the midst of all that death, He introduces *life*. Where the Spirit of life introduces life, there is the Church. The kind of life He instigates is contagious, and so from the beginning it has spread.

It has spread despite every attempt to stop it. Those attempts consist of two main techniques—the enemy wants either to crush it or corrupt it. The initial response is to lash out in hatred. If the frontal assault doesn't work, if persecution doesn't exterminate the Church, then the technique is to move on to corruption. Elimination is best, but corruption will do almost as well.

But God has not just set life loose in the world. He has set immortal life loose in the world, resurrection life loose in the world, divine life loose in the world. It can be smashed, but like quicksilver it scatters everywhere. And when it has been scattered everywhere, it begins to grow and multiply from there.

This Church is a body, and is attached to her head, who is the Lord Jesus. The body identifies itself as gathering to Jesus by gathering around one Bible and two sacraments. That which defines the Church is Word and sacrament; that which creates the Church is everlasting life given by the Spirit.

When it comes to sharing in this life, denominations are not really a barrier. They are a trifle really—believers from different communions routinely recognize one another, fellowship together, work together, and pray together. And two people at odds with one another, members of the same Church hating one another across the distance of just a few pews, might have no experience of this shared life. Denominations don't create this unity. They may be used by the Spirit to help keep some kind of order, but they are not the ground of unity. Christ is the ground of unity.

When the apostle tells us to labor to preserve the unity of the Spirit in the bond of peace, he is assuming that there is a unity that we already possess, a unity that is just given to us by grace. Every true Christian already has it with every true Christian. It can be disrupted, certainly—which is why he takes the trouble to warn us to work at not disrupting it. But the unity itself is not an accomplishment of ours. We do not accomplish anything in this regard, except in successfully avoiding all temptations to wreck it.

How would we wreck it? If a certain kind of unity is simply given to the Church, then our duty is to work at preserving the unity of the Spirit in the bond of peace. Our task here is maintenance. If we are given unity, then we seek to avoid those sins against charity that would cause Christians to let go of what they have. Thus sins like envy, or malice, or backbiting, or pride, would be the sins we could commit that would be bad for the given unity.

But there is another kind of unity, the kind we are not *supposed* to have yet. We are all supposed to grow up into the unity of the faith, into the perfect man. The history of the world is a history of maturation. When God placed Adam and Eve in the Garden, it was a local Garden that had been established by God—God gave us a foothold of tamed space, a beachhead of groomed paths. But the rest of the world was wild, and needed to be transformed into a Garden planet.

Once sin entered the world, it became a story of interrupted maturation, restoration, and then resumed maturation. The mission has always been to tame the planet, to make it flourish, not in a wild state, but as a luxuriant garden. That mission got more difficult because of our fall into sin, but the mission was never aborted because of sin.

The assignment to subdue the earth, to replenish it, was the fundamental cultural mandate. It was given to mankind before the Fall. But right after the Flood, which was a massive judgment on worldwide sin, God reissues the cultural mandate, using many of the same phrases. Man was told to subdue the world before he fell into sin, and he was told to do it after he fell into sin. Clearly the sin gets in the way and has to be addressed. Not only so, but we were incapable of addressing it on our own. *That* had to be done by the Messiah. But the fact that we could not fulfill the cultural mandate did not mean that God had in any way abrogated the cultural mandate.

This means that once the issue of sin has been addressed, and the resultant power of death over us all, it is possible for mankind to grow up to maturity, but this time in Christ. Outside of Christ, we remain in the first Adam, perpetually stuck in our sin and rebellion and consequential immaturity.

But when we are introduced to Christ, when we are brought into Christ, maturity does not arrive instantly. Of course not. But maturity in Christ is now a *possibility*. And this is why the cultural mandate originally given to Adam and Eve, and which was reiterated to Noah, is now reaffirmed again, this time in what is called the Great Commission. In that Commission, the Church is told to do some very striking things.

Remember that man was given dominion over the world, and that dominion was never revoked. Sin took dominion over man, and that crippled him in his ability to fulfill the cultural mandate. The gospel—the message of the death, burial, and resurrection of Jesus—takes dominion in principle over sin. Man in Adam cannot fulfill the mandate that is still his, but man in Christ can do so. All who believe in Jesus Christ are ushered into a new humanity, a humanity that retains the cultural mandate, but has been restored in its ability to fulfill it. And this is why the language of the Great Commission is so important.

Jesus said that all authority in Heaven and on earth has been given to Him. That is the groundwork for the commission. He then says that His followers are to *therefore* go. It is not enough to go. We must *therefore* go. We must go and do as we have been instructed *because* Jesus has all authority in Heaven and on earth.

And when we go, what are we instructed to do? The business of the Church—which is the object of this chapter—consists of two things: birth and growth. Jesus said that we were to "therefore go," and to "disciple the nations." What follows after that is a description of that task—we are to disciple the nations by baptizing them and teaching them to obey everything Jesus taught.

This is quite a radical task. Jesus didn't say most of the nations, or some of the people in some of the nations, but rather to "disciple the nations." The direct object of the verb is *ethnoi*, nations. We were to undertake this task because Jesus has been given all authority in Heaven and on earth. The things we are to do as we disciple the nations are to "baptize" and to "teach."

Now if the human race has been remade in Christ, and if that new human race has been given the cultural mandate again, along with the power of completing it, then this means that the future is necessarily Christian. If God's intention from the beginning was for the earth to be transformed into a Garden City, and this is the vision for the earth we are given with the images of Church and Garden City blending together, what are we to make of it?

The Church is described as the New Jerusalem in numerous places. In Revelation, the angel tells John that he will show him the bride, the wife of the Lamb. And who is the bride of Christ? The Church. And having said this, he took John to a high mountain and showed him the New Jerusalem, descending down the central aisle.

Christians are told in the book of Hebrews that they have not come to a mountain that can be touched, but that they have come to a heavenly Jerusalem, which is what happens in every worship service. The apostle Paul says in the book of Galatians that the Jerusalem above is the mother of us all. At the climax of history, the kings of the earth are said to bring their honor and glory into the New Jerusalem, which is the Church.

If all these things are brought together, we see that the Church is not a staging area for an expedition to the heavenly places. It is a staging area, certainly, but the movement is to be the other way. In the Lord's Prayer, Jesus taught His disciples to pray "Thy kingdom come," not "Thy kingdom go," and the prayer went on to ask for God's will to be done "on earth as it is in Heaven." It is not "Thy will be done in Heaven when we get there."

The only thing that remains is to reconcile this high view of the Church, found throughout all Scripture, with the mundane realities we encounter down here. There is the Church, and then there are *churches*.

A little boy once famously defined faith as "believing what you know ain't so." It is tempting to say that any exercise that attempts to use the lofty language of the Scripture with regard to the Church (the bride of the Lamb, without spot or wrinkle, the mother of us all, the New Jerusalem, etc.) about the motley gaggle of people renting space in some store front, sitting on folding chairs, and singing out of tune half the time is an exercise that is doing precisely this—trying to believe what you know ain't so.

This focus on the inchoate state of the Church you actually have to *attend* neglects the importance of history and time. The soaring rhetoric of Scripture when it comes to the Church is rhetoric that usually speaks of what the Church is in the process of becoming. If we were there already, we wouldn't be having the discussion. The vision cast in Scripture is a vision of the future—and not an attempt to say something like, "Who are you going to believe? Me, or your lying eyes?"

History is full of seed. The field is the world, and the Word is sown in the world. Some is choked with weeds, and some is snatched by the birds of the air. But much of it falls on good soil, and bears a true crop. But when you look at a small plant, shooting up through the soil, you need to do more than look *at* it. Rather, the need is to look *along* its story, looking through time to the harvest.

We are not to despise the day of small beginnings. A future Miss America was once a single cell, and a ferocious linebacker in the NFL was the same thing, a single cell, and about the same size—maybe smaller. We are to evaluate the beginning by the end, and not the other way around.

So when we talk about the Church, we have to distinguish the Church in history from the Church at the end of history. We have to mark the difference between the historical Church and the eschatological Church. If the Church at the end of history, the eschatological Church, will be without spot or wrinkle or any such blemish, it is not hard to reason backwards to conclude that the historical church has spots, wrinkles, and blemishes.

And sure enough, it does. We have church splits, and lame worship services, and aberrant doctrine, and women preaching, and not enough pancake batter at the men's prayer breakfast. We have church architecture that wants to blend in with the mall, and preachers who want to be celebrities, and retreatist theologies to hide our disobedience in.

This is what seed looks like, and it spends a lot of time in the dirt.

But we should spend less time looking at the Church (whatever moment we choose to look), and more time looking along the Church. We should look at the video, not the snapshot. We should look back along the line at the very unpromising beginnings—eleven blue collar workers standing on a mountain outside Jerusalem— look at where we are now, and then look along the line of the future as we anticipate the coming glory. Eye has not seen and ear has not heard what God has prepared for those who love Him.

This is how we learn not to despise the day of small beginnings. The end is contained in the beginning, but only the eye of faith can see it there. Like a great composer, God reiterates His themes and weaves them through all that He does. We saw in our discussion of creation that when the world was fresh and innocent, it was also immature. That was a design feature. God loves infants and infancy.

He loves it especially when we think we are more grown up than we actually are, because He knows how embarrassed about it we will be later on. But He is not embarrassed. He is not ashamed to call us His brothers. We are His little brothers, but we are the little brothers that God has big plans for.

Faith in the present is what summons forth a particular future. When God promised all the nations to Abraham—when God promised the Church to Abraham—there was not a lot for Abraham to go on if all he had were the newspapers. He came from a sophisticated city, Ur of the Chaldees, and he went out to live a nomadic existence in tents. Apart from the land he bought for the burial of his wife, he did not inherit the land he was walking on. And yet he rejoiced to see the day of the Lord Jesus; he saw it and was glad.

Because he saw it when it wasn't there, he made it possible for us to see it now that it is here. And when we see what is not yet here, we make it possible for what is not yet here to arrive. What is it that overcomes the world? Is it not our faith? When we look along the history of the Church, seeing the end result by viewing it in and through the promises of God, we become the instrument for bringing about that glorious culmination.

If we love the Church as she now is, we will love her into the Church that has been promised us.

THE FINAL THINGS

WE LIKE TO LIVE WITH THE FALSE COM-
fort of thinking that the "final" things are always many
eons away. When someone uses the word *eschatology*, we
often think of something remote, off in the distant future. But that word *eschatology* can be used in two senses.
One has to do with the final events in the history of
our planet, but the other has to do with the ultimate
issues which confront every man and every woman—and
which actually confront us daily. These are the questions
that every thinking person should ask himself, even if it
is sometimes only in the middle of a sleepless night at
around two in the morning.

These are the questions of Heaven and Hell, and the
actual spiritual condition of each individual when he
dies. However far off the end of the world is, the end

of the world as far as *I* am concerned is something that can be guessed with a fair degree of accuracy by a life insurance company. However soon it will be that all the nations of men will be assembled before their Maker, it is fairly certain that I will be summoned to His presence in something under 40 years. It may be longer than that for you, and of course it may be shorter. It could be a matter of hours.

But the end of the whole world is largely an *academic* question for each individual. It certainly matters for them in one sense, but most of the world's population will actually go to meet God one by one. This is not a fire drill, where the whole school evacuates and is standing out in the parking lot. No, most of us are going to be called to the principal's office one at a time. And as soon as the door out to the hallway closes behind him, we all sit quietly for a moment, and then start squirreling around again.

The day we get expelled and the day they tear the school down are related in some ways to this same question, but they are not exactly the same thing.

In an earlier chapter we discussed how every sin is Hell in microcosm. Some engravers have managed to get the Lord's Prayer onto the head of a pin. God has the library that dictates the physical specs for a human being contained within the DNA library that fits inside a single cell. These are triumphs of miniaturization, but the devil can do it also. All the emptiness and hollowness of the outer darkness is contained, in principle, at the heart of every sin.

If absolutely everything is going to be put right, with no remainder, this means that every person will have to find a final place that *fits*. And in order for something to fit, it must be fitting, and before that can be, it must be fitted. And—given the bent and twisted nature of our race—only two things are finally fitting, which are justice and mercy.

All of us finally become what we are becoming, and this means that when we have *arrived*, we will fit where we have arrived. We eventually get there, and nothing will be sticking out. Vessels of mercy are fitted for mercy, and vessels of wrath are fitted for destruction.

Not one shed tear will be out of place. All the tears will have been collected in a bottle by God. Not one wound will be unhealed, and not one scar will be left. No injustice will remain to rankle, and all manner of things shall be well. Not one ingrate will remain within the city, and not one mongrel dog will roam the golden streets. Everything will be right where it ought to be, right where it needs to be. Everything will be exactly where it *has* to be.

But in order to fit then, we must be fitted now. We sometimes wonder why God doesn't make it more obvious that this is what He is doing, but remember that when Solomon built the Temple, there was no sound of the chisel on the site (1 Kings 6:7). God is fitting us for our final place, and we are not quite sure how He is doing it. We think there ought to be power tools, but we can't hear any power tools. We look around and see what we think are "our lives," and the lives of those around us. But all of this is God's workbench.

We are the stonework for this great house that is being built, and we are being "built up" into it (1 Pet. 2:5). As the Authorized Version puts it elsewhere, we are being "fitly framed" as we are being placed in that building (Eph. 2:21). But the images in both those passages are a combination of organic growth and straight-up construction. We are stones, but we are living stones. We are being fitly framed into the wall, but we also *grow* up into a "holy temple."

Moving in the contrary direction, to be fitted for the Abyss doesn't take much. The shapelessness of narcissism can go absolutely anywhere in the void, but to be fitted for the glories of Heaven requires the perfect hand of the perfect artisan. This is because Heaven *works*. That shapeless landfill, the one with fires scattered all over, riddled with worms, doesn't have to work. Nothing has to fit, and so any kind of shapeless "fitting" will do. Gehenna, the landfill outside Jerusalem, was one of the early pictures of this Hell.

It is this sense of eschatology that deals with the "four last things"—death, judgment, Hell, and Heaven. Every man will die, every man will be evaluated and evaluated perfectly, and every man will be assigned his final destination. When that last assignment is registered, there will be no argument, there will be nothing to say. The Bible says that every mouth will be stopped.

The Lord Jesus is the One through whom the world will be judged, and as He is the Word of God, it is fitting that He be considered the Last Word. That Last Word will be pronounced at the Last Day, and that Last Day will contain the summation of all the last things. The judgment is going to be the denouement of a great novel, and in that final chapter every thread will be picked up and resolved. There will be no critics sitting in judgment on that novel, no one judging the judgment, but if there were, there would be no fault that could be found in it.

In our glib and sophomoric tendencies to judge the God of the whole earth, we sometimes act as though the Final Judgment is an indictment on the justice of God. But how could it be an indictment on the justice of God when it *is* the justice of God?

The human heart is deceitfully wicked, and slippery as well. It is so slippery that it wants an indictment against the justice of the process that will bring nothing but inexorable and necessary justice to bear on every word and action. Justice is the judge, and we want justice to be the defendant. God is the judge, and to use that wonderful phrase by Lewis, we want God in the dock. We have an emotional problem with Hell, not a theological problem. We want grace and mercy to be *owed* to us, but if it were owed, it wouldn't be grace or mercy. And the theological problem that we *do* have—that of sinners being able to come into the presence of a holy God—is a problem that was only solved by God sounding the depth of His own wisdom. The problem of unjust sinners communing with a holy God is a problem that was solved by the mystery of the God/man dying on a tree just a short walk outside Jerusalem. Such a striking solution was called for because it was a striking problem.

Throwing people who richly deserve it into the outer darkness is not a striking problem. It presents an emotional problem for those who are threatened by it, and so they will say all kinds of crazy things in order to get Christians to keep quiet about things like the Final Judgment. One of those things is the idea that the final hammer fall of justice is somehow going to be unjust.

Suppose for a moment that God placed an invisible recording device around the neck of every last person, and this recording device was designed to record only those statements that consisted of moral evaluations of other people. Suppose further that God took these recordings from around the necks of all of us, distilled from those judgments we had made of others a moral code, and then judged each one of us by that moral code. How would all of us fare? To ask the question is to answer it.

So then we know what justice is—for we rigorously apply the standards of it all the day long to others—but we cannot pretend that we ourselves live up to those standards. If God were to simply weigh us in the scales that we have fashioned for everyone else, then all of us would be found drastically wanting. Every word, every thought, every gesture is evaluated a certain way for all outbound traffic and another way for all inbound traffic. The phrase for this is "double standards."

And so what will happen when all double standards are blown away like smoke in a gale? For the damned, the cosmos will become tiny and the ego large in comparison, because the gnawing ego will try to gather everything into it. The ego will not be large, but it will *feel* large. It will feel like everything. For the saved, the cosmos will hurtle away from him into greater and greater immensities, and the ego will be humbled, will feel small in comparison. And when the human heart is humbled in this way, it will be lifted up. It will grow and mature, and will enter into its own estate, its own majority, its own joy.

The final things means closure—closure in one sense, and an infinite opening in another. Damnation is the final and complete turn inward—*incurvatus in se*. The soul turns in upon itself and ultimately winds up devouring itself. Salvation is when the soul is reunited with the body, and turned loose to adore God and enjoy Him forever. That redeemed soul faces *out*. The world, and the oceans, and the starry heavens, and the planets, and the trackless forests, and the emerald cities filled with redeemed humanity, all lie before him. There will be nothing to do but sing to God and *explore*.

That marvelous phrase that Lewis used to describe what this is like is almost perfect. "Further up and further in." The more we grow and mature, the greater God will seem to us. He is not growing, for He is already infinite. Christ is not maturing, for He is the perfect man that we are going to be growing up into forever. But as we grow, we will understand more. As we grow, our capacity for joy will increase.

And this, incidentally, solves a problem that has sometimes vexed humble Christians—the whole problem of "rewards." It is undeniable that Scripture offers us rewards at the resurrection, and some of them are decked out in the most fantastic imagery. And yet, taken a certain way, it doesn't seem right somehow. Why should we be motivated to love and good deeds down here because we have been enticed with a chest full of celestial doubloons up there? Isn't that kind of *mercenary*? Doesn't it kind of defeat the whole point of Heaven?

And yet, we are taught in unmistakable terms that God will reward each man according to what he has done. How are we to reconcile this and make every man's reception of his reward consistent with love and humility? There will be no swank in Heaven.

Picture it this way. Think of the love of God as a vast infinite ocean, an ocean of liquefied light. Our resurrection bodies are containers that have been specially fashioned to be able to hold it—to hold it in fullness, and without any leakage whatever. Now there is nothing mercenary about it if we discover that some saints lived and loved in such a way that when they came to the resurrection, they were a quart jar. Others were a gallon, and others were five gallons. The apostle Paul, when he arrived, was a fifty gallon drum.

What is the difference between these containers? In one sense, nothing. They are all filled to the brim with the same thing. They all experience the maximum delight that they can experience. But some, because of how they have grown in grace, have *a larger capacity for joy*. Their heart was enlarged. And where they currently are, the little half-pint Christians will soon enough be. But when they get there, the others will be farther on by that point, but that's all right. This is not a footrace. Further up and further in.

And then, if we stop for a moment to think about it, when you compare a pint to an infinite ocean of joy, and then compare a fifty gallon drum to that same in-finite ocean of joy, the difference in the ratios doesn't leave any room for comparisons. And so because all are full and overflowing, there will be no comparisons, and if there were to be comparisons, they wouldn't really be possible. They wouldn't mean anything. Six inches compared to infinity does not have very much over three inches compared to infinity.

As mentioned before, it is no competition. There is no envy there, no scratching or clawing. That means that every redeemed soul will be delighted beyond measure by every redeemed soul who is ahead of him. "Don't you wish you had more joy, the way he has up there?" "But I don't have room for it . . . I am full *now*. But I will have more room shortly, and then I will be even more full." "But he will still be ahead of you." "I know. Isn't it glorious?"

Salvation is not about getting into the swankest coun-try club ever. It is not about manicured lawns, or drink-ing 80 proof ambrosia out of crystal cups. It is about the relationship between God and man, and obviously this is not possible if God does not exist. But it is not observed often enough that this salvation is impossible if *man* does not exist. This is another way of posing the same question that is raised in C.S. Lewis's great novel, *Till We Have Faces*. How can we meet the gods face to face till we have faces?

God does not need to come into being so that we
may be with Him. *Man* needs to come into being so that
God might be with us. We are shapeless in our sins, and
we need to be shaped into the new man. We are inchoate in our confusions, and we need to be gathered up
into the ordered beauty of the new creation. The Lord
says that He makes all things new.

So as we look forward to our salvation—as we certainly ought to be doing—we ought not to think of it as "people going to Heaven." It is better described as the hard-
edged definitions of Heaven coming down into this
murky place and beginning the long process of bringing
us into focus. People don't go to Heaven. Heaven comes
and gets us. This is the meaning of that great name for
the Lord Jesus, *Immanuel*. God with us.

An old blues song laments that everyone wants to
go to Heaven, but nobody wants to die. It is worse than
that. Everybody wants to go to Heaven, but absolutely
no one wants it to come here. If Heaven comes down, it
might start messing with things.

As our bodies fall apart—which they do because of
sin—a different process entirely is going on inside us.
Though the outer man is wasting away, due to the Fall,
our inner man is being renewed day after day. What is it
being renewed *for*?

Heaven comes down to men before men go up into
Heaven. We pray as the Lord taught us, and that means

that we pray for the kingdom to come. We do not pray that the kingdom might *go*. Salvation, in order for it to occur at all, has to be a salvation that *fetches* us.

This is just another way of noticing that this necessitates a salvation that is by grace alone. In other words, when we think of salvation as gilt sky castles, where we are all fed succulent grapes the size of plums, it is—ironically—something we will think we have somehow earned. But when we see salvation straight on, rightly, we know that it is a gift. When Heaven begins work on us here, when Jesus carries us into His workshop to place us on the workbench of this world, He does it because He intends to work humility into us.

Apart from that, if we were taken straightway to Heaven, we would all think that we had somehow won a contest. We would think we had taken the prize, brought home the laurels. But salvation is always configured so that no one can boast, and it takes a good bit of trying to be holy in this world to knock the boasting out of us.

Failures can be really bracing.

THE CREED IN A NUTSHELL

I BELIEVE . . . GENUINE CHRISTIAN EX-
perience begins with faith, continues in faith, and ends
in faith. The just shall live by faith. What is it that overcomes the world? Is it not our faith? The earliest of the
great Christian creeds begins with the great biblical truth
of faith alone.

I believe in God . . . | Our faith is not faith in faith,
or trust in the virtues of believing. The act of loyal faith
looks outward, away from itself. Eyes were not made to
look at themselves, but rather at the world. The verb to
believe requires an object, and Christian belief is foundationally belief in God.

I believe in God the Father | We do not believe in a
generic force or absolute vanilla-deity-like substance. We
believe in God the Father. His relationship to His Son is

utterly and infinitely personal. He is the eternal *Father*. Because we believe in Him, this means that we believe that fatherhood is the ultimate font of all things, the ultimate reality. His Fatherhood is an essential part of His being—He exists necessarily, and He exists as a Father.

Almighty | God is the Almighty God. His power and strength are infinite, His omnipotence is bounded by nothing other than His own nature and character. This means that His omnipotence cannot be insulted by pitching it against itself, as though nonsense could become something else if God Almighty simply decreed it. God can do absolutely anything that is consistent with who He has always been.

Maker of Heaven and Earth | Our faith in God, and our knowledge of Him, begins with the understanding that He is our Father. We confess secondly that He is Almighty. In the third place, we believe that He is the absolute Maker of every contingent thing. We kneel before the Lord our Maker. We do not belong to ourselves because we did not make ourselves. Our existence is dependent upon the will of someone outside ourselves, and it is to Him that we owe every debt of thanks. He is our Maker.

And in | From the very beginning, faithful Christians have held to the importance of those words *and in*. But we do not believe in a Jesus who is *alongside* God, but rather in a Jesus who brings us to God. If we have seen

Him, we have seen the Father. The Word was God and the Word was with God.

And in Jesus Christ | Jesus is descended from David the king, and He is the promised Messiah, the Christ. He grew up in Nazareth, and His name means that He will save His people from their sins. As the Christ, He was the fulfillment of centuries of promise.

His only begotten Son | Jesus Christ did not have a human father—He was conceived in the womb of His mother Mary apart from any human agency. He was carried by Mary, but begotten by God.

Our Lord. | Fully human, fully divine, the Lord Jesus is *necessarily* Lord. It is not possible to recognize in Him the Savior of the human race without simultaneously recognizing in Him the Lord of us all.

He was conceived by the Holy Ghost | The Holy Spirit overshadowed Mary, which means that it is fully appropriate to call the Lord Jesus the Son of God. He is the only begotten Son of God, which means He is fully God. While He had no human father, He had a human grandfather on His mother's side. He was born of a woman in exactly the same way every human being since Cain has come into the world. His full humanity is beyond all doubt.

And born of the virgin, Mary. | Mary is the only woman in the history of the world to have given birth without having known a man. Not only does this indicate the uniqueness of Jesus, it also is the reason why it was possible for Him to be a true human, descended from Adam in truth, and yet to be without sin. A virgin birth is necessary if there is to be no human father, for it is the human father that passes on the covenantal burden of our sinfulness.

He suffered under Pontius Pilate, was crucified, died, and was buried. | The sufferings of Christ were historical, and so it is that this foundational confession of Christian belief contains the name of a provincial prefect appointed by the emperor Tiberius. During the time of Pilate's rule, the Lord Jesus was crucified, died on the cross, and then was buried.

He descended into Hades. | In the Greek of the Creed, the word here is Hades, not Hell. Hades was the place of the departed dead—the Hebrew word for it was Sheol—and was not the place of final damnation, not the lake of fire. The forms of the Creed that say *He descended into Hell* are therefore misleading.

On the third day He rose again, from the dead, | The plot against the Lord Jesus appeared to have gone perfectly, and the only thing that ruined it was that Jesus came back from the dead. And when that happened, the whole world was made new.

Ascended into Heaven, and sits at the right hand of God the Father Almighty | After appearing to His overjoyed disciples over the course of a number of weeks, instructing

them on the meaning of all the Scriptures that had anticipated this turn of events, the Lord Jesus ascended into
the heavens. He disappeared from the sight of the disciples, and appeared in the throne room of the Ancient
of Days, where He was seated at the right hand of God,
and where He was given universal dominion over all the
nations of men (Eph. 1:20-22).

From thence He will come to judge the living and the dead.
| Having been seated at the right hand of God, He has
been invited to rule from that place until all His enemies
have been made His footstool (Heb. 1:13, 10:13). When
all of them have been subdued, with the solitary excep-
tion of death itself, He will rise up from His throne and
will come back to earth in order to judge both the living
and the dead.

I believe in the Holy Ghost | Christian faith is faith in
the Father, faith in the Son, and faith in the Holy Spirit
of both Father and Son. This Spirit is as personal as the
Father and the Son, and so this tri-personal God is the
object of our trust. We believe in one God, Father, Son,
and Spirit.

The holy catholic Church | The universal Church is
formed by the Holy Spirit. Animated by the Spirit of
Christ, the Christian Church is therefore the body of
Christ.

The communion of saints | As a result of the Spirit's
work, all the saints of God have true fellowship, true

communion together. The redeemed of God have been made into one organism, and because they partake of God by faith, they necessarily partake of one another.

The forgiveness of sins | Apart from the forgiveness of sin, the flawed material of humankind could not partake in any of this. But because Christ died and rose, we believe in (and truly experience) the forgiveness of sins.

The resurrection of the body | Forgiveness of sins means that we have died with Christ. Walking in newness of life means that we are anticipating the resurrection in our earthly lives. And when the time of the consummation of all things arrives, our bodies will be resurrected in just the same way that the body of Jesus was resurrected. We believe that this will happen, and so we confess our faith that it will.

And the life everlasting. | And so it is that we will live forever in Christ. Having partaken of His death, we are privileged to have been made partakers of His everlasting life.

Amen. | Amen and amen.

EPILOGUE

THE CHRISTIAN FAITH GIVES AN AC-
count of the world, and from what you have read thus
far, you can see that I believe it gives a true account of
the world. The Christian faith certainly has an effect on
the hearts of men, but it is too large to be entirely contained within the hearts of men. In other words, it is either true or it is not true. It cannot be true just "for us."

If the facts recounted by the writers of Scripture are
not in fact true, if they do not correspond with the way
that things actually are out in the world of history, science, journalism, psychology, and so on, then—as the
apostle Paul once put it—we Christians of all men are
most to be pitied (1 Cor. 15:19). If it is only good for
our faith community, this is just another way of saying
that it is good for nothing.

If Jesus did not come back from the dead, then we will not do so either. The apostle said that the only rational response to this would be to eat, drink and be merry because the death that will never cease will descend on us the next day (1 Cor. 15:32). But if He *did* come back from death, then the world cannot be viewed in the same way ever again. Behold, He makes all things new. And just because He *did* return from death, the news of that enables Christians to invite nonbelievers to come and taste, come and see.

This message of salvation is honey made by industrious celestial bees, and they work in fields of clover the size of Jupiter. There is more than enough for you. This offer of the gospel places just a bit of it on the tip of your tongue. *There*—do you taste it now? The Spirit and the Bride say *come*.